THE DO-IT-YOURSELF GUIDE TO SURVIVING THE
ZOMBIE
APOCALYPSE

By
Bud Hanzel and John Olson

Illustrated by
Mark Stegbauer

HANSON PRESS
Redwing • Minnesota

For Ian who hoped.

For Hayley who wished.

And for Brenna who always believed.

J.O.

For my Lord, Jesus Christ, who made it happen.

For my sisters, Tina and Edie who hoped and prayed for it to happen.

*For my parents, Rick and Trudy and sister, Lisa
who didn't live to see it happen.*

And for my friend and brother Paul, who knew it all the time.

B.H.

For my family, who encouraged me to dream.

For my friends, who helped me make them come true

M.S.

ACKNOWLEDGEMENTS

The authors would like to acknowledge and thank the following
individuals for their contributions (either known, or unknown)
to this project:

Tom Allison
David Arnold
Ray Ballinger
Carl Borg
Brenna Olson
Hayley Olson
Ian Olson
Paul Olson
Pamela Ligget-Olson
Nick Post
Landen Schooler
Burl Zorn

We cannot thank you enough for your support
and encouragement throughout the creative process.

TABLE OF CONTENTS

APPENDICES

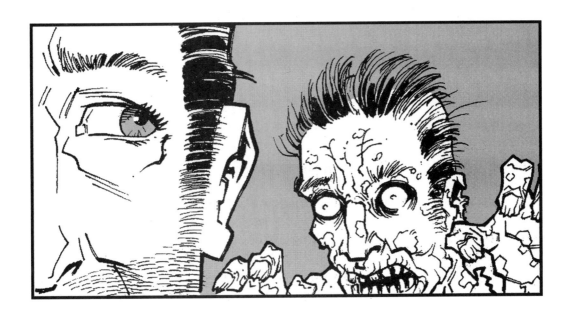

INTRODUCTION

It's going to happen… you know it is. One day, sooner than we expect, something is going to go very wrong. Why should we worry about global warming, economic meltdown, wars in the Middle East, Third World dictators in possession of nuclear weapons, or a bunch of fascist rag-heads whose religion dictates that they kill the infidels (that's us by-the-way. You know, everybody who isn't them), when the true threat to our existence is an event so unspeakably catastrophic that all other human proclivities toward self-destruction pale by comparison. The reality of the ultimate downfall of modern man lies in the veiled truths of the Hollywood machine; small fictional glimpses of an event so frightening that it has to be wrapped in humor for the masses to even look at it.

You, as the cultured consumer of quality literature, discerning viewer of finer works of cinematography, and the purchaser of this ultimate self-help tome (you did buy it right?*) obviously understand that the human race exists on the brink of disaster. Our demise is imminent, and it seems particularly clear to those of us with any refined vision that we are just one mutated virus, military experiment, rogue comet, or mysterious green mist away from a full-blown zombie apocalypse.

* If you haven't bought it yet, you should stop reading and in the fine tradition of American capitalism, cough up a few of those hard earned bucks.

Therefore, the need for this manual is abundantly clear. In fact, it is well over due. When the zombies rise (and you know they will), you want to be prepared, you want to have a plan, you want to protect yourself. You want to have the peace of mind knowing that you have done everything you can to ensure your survival and that of your friends and family. In short, you want to have read this book and followed its instructions.

There have been other works on this subject, some more exhaustive, but none so consistently focused on your survival, so practical in their advice, so clearly aimed at what you really need to know as to give you the peace of mind that when the worst happens, the outcome is truly in your own hands, mind, and will to survive.

In easy-to-follow chapters, the authors of this extraordinary volume have set forth clear instructions that will ensure your survival in the impending zombie apocalypse. We have covered such areas of concern as what you need to know about zombies, what weapons make the best choices for sustained survival, what supplies and equipment are necessary, when it is advisable (or not) to travel, and in general, how to deal with the most fearsome disaster to ever befall the human race. In fact, we, the authors, are so confident in the clarity of our vision on the matter that we are offering you an incredible iron clad guarantee: If you purchase this book and fully heed its advice, you will survive the zombie apocalypse or we will double your money back.

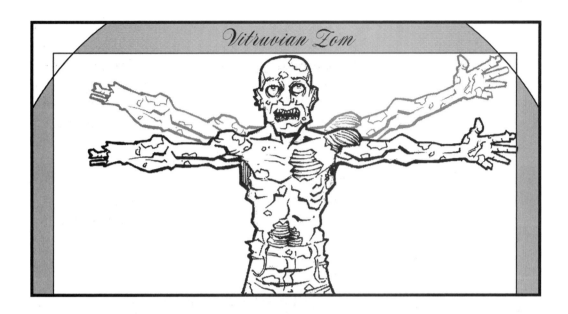

Vitruvian Zom

CHAPTER 1: ZOMBOLOGY 101

Everything you need to know about zombies.

Zombie: The body of a dead person given the semblance of life.

The origins of zombies arise from the Voodoo beliefs first practiced in Africa, and later transplanted to Haiti, Brazil, the Caribbean Islands, and even areas in the Southern United States. In Voodoo practices, newly dead people could be animated through supernatural means. These zombies were usually intended to exact some revenge upon a specific person or group and posed little or no danger to individuals outside of their intended victims. While these old-world zombies were highly feared creatures, they were hardly the worldwide threat to humanity that modern zombies represent. The biggest single

Typical old world zombie.

3

Modern zombie.

characteristic that old-world and modern zombies have in common is, of course, the fact that they are dead.

Modern zombies are the result of… well; wait that really doesn't matter much does it? When the zombies rise, you are not very likely to be certain of the cause (kind of like the swine flu), so it is hardly need-to-know information. It is far more important that you understand certain zombie facts so that you can best understand the zombie threat.

First, zombies, by definition are dead; some catalyzing agent has re-animated their bodies. Regardless of the means of transformation, modern zombies are once living humans who have become decaying, animated corpses, intent on finding and consuming all remaining human flesh (which, of course, means you).

The biggest advantage you have over the zombies is that you are alive and they are not.

THE ZOMBIE PARADOX: LIVING THE UN-LIFE

As already stated, zombies are dead. So, how do they continue to move about? The answer is in the Zombie Transforming Agent (ZTA), which animates the corpses. Regardless of the source or specifics of the ZTA (a rogue, mutated, or genetically engineered virus or some combination thereof is the most likely candidate), the effects will be generally the same. The ZTA, in "infecting" the host, permeates every cell of the host's body. This causes a disruption of normal cellular processes and results in the death of the human host. The host's death is clinical and spiritual, but not a complete biological death. Instead, a transformation occurs, which allows the body's cells to relate according to the dictates of the ZTA. Essentially the human host's spirit is forcibly evicted from the body, leaving nothing but a dying biological husk. The ZTA sets up shop with its own agenda, and none of the essence of the person remains.

You must remember that a zombie is a zombie, even when it's your mom. Do not allow yourself to believe for a moment that anything of the host is left behind. The created zombie is a different creature entirely, operating by its own set of biological instincts. Whatever biological life remains is purely a function of the ZTA itself and is subject to its own particular requirements for survival. What truly makes these new creatures zombies is the fact that their major bodily functions cease, they no longer breathe or

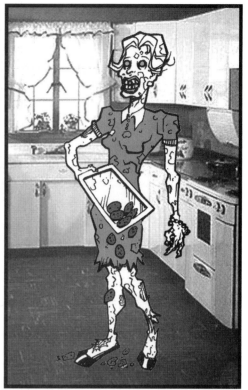

Anyone's mom can be a zombie.

have a heartbeat, and their digestive systems have shut down almost completely. Deprived of these life-sustaining bodily functions, their tissues simply begin to desiccate and decay.

The paradox is that by biological standards, some life remains within the body of a zombie, but it has absolutely nothing to do with the former life of the human host.

While cursorily similar, the process of becoming a zombie is not to be confused with the process of becoming a Hollywood actress, New York runway model, or a Washington politician.

ZOMNAMBULATION: FROM SPRINTING MANIAC TO SHAMBLING HEAP

More recent movie portrayals of zombies have created a debate regarding zombie movement. Never fear, we are here to iron out the wrinkles and help you understand what will or will not be the case.

Obviously, a fast moving, highly aggressive, motor-coordinated zombie is a far greater threat to your well being than the lumbering, shuffling hordes. So, which is it to be? Unfortunately, the answer, when it comes to zomnabulation, is some from column A and some from column B.

Remember, as has been reiterated already numerous times, zombies are dead. (Notice the pattern here?) While the ZTA has hijacked the host's body, various tissues are still subject to deterioration and such mundane factors as environment and gravity. The ZTA uses the nervous system as a primary control conduit for the body, but their rate of decay will determine the responsiveness of the outlying tissues.

Another feature of the zombie transformation is that the ZTA, in order to overcome certain processes, such as rigor mortis, floods the body's cells with a substance that has the effect of slowing normal cellular breakdown. This substance will logically serve as an anti-coagulant as well, so the blood does not thicken in the body, impeding movement.

Without a beating heart to circulate blood throughout the body, all that thinned blood will pool in the lower extremities. This in itself will tend to hinder movement as it hastens the breakdown of normal tissues. It is also responsible for swelling and the appearance of purple blotches and blood blisters on zombies, usually occurring below the torso and on the hands and lower arms.

So what about running zombies, you ask? (We're getting to that.) When a human body dies, the brain cells are the first cells to experience biological death. These are the very cells, which the ZTA has taken over, and which allow it to command the body and are central to its

Sprinting maniac zombie.

survival within the host. (The ZTA Command Center if you will.) Under normal conditions, other cells in the body, particularly muscle, bone, and connective tissues, may not experience cellular breakdown for as long as seventy-two hours after death.

From the moment the ZTA has taken over the host body entirely, its very existence is on a sharp decline. As the muscles may remain "alive" for as long as seventy-two hours, the mobility of the zombie is very high in its first hours. Zombies will be able to run, grasp, jump, even grapple with an acuity not dissimilar to the normal abilities of the specific human body.

A few factors govern just how long a zombie retains its motility. It has been stated that certain tissues may not experience cellular breakdown for as long as seventy-two hours after death. This period is considerably shortened by activity, as the cells consume the available oxygen and other essential chemical resources. Once the cells resources have been consumed, biological death will occur, and the zombie will then be dependent on the ZTA's unique ability to override the chemistry of death and force the cells to continue to function, until such time that the cell walls themselves rupture under the strain of operation.

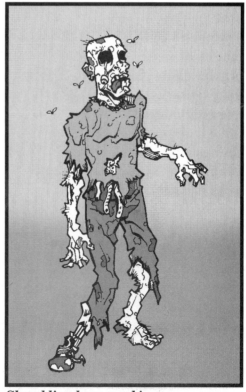

Exactly how active a zombie is depends on its rate of success at obtaining sustenance and a few environmental factors, such as temperature and humidity. These factors will all combine to determine its exact mobility. This is a critical point to understand and accounts for why the spread of the zombies occurs at such an accelerated pace.

So, the short answer is, "yes," zombies can run, but only for about twenty-four to seventy-two hours following the host's death and the rise into un-life.

Shambling heap zombie.

Thereafter, the zombie's mobility will steadily and rapidly decrease, transforming the animated corpse from a fast moving, frantic, survival-driven maniac, into a halting, slow moving, uncoordinated, but no less persistent, heap.

ZOMBIE SURVIVAL: UN-LIFE EXPECTANCY

From the moment of transformation, the ZTA is driven solely on a biologically instinctive level to pursue its own survival. There is no intelligence or consciousness at work, only a relentless pursuit of what is necessary for it own continuation.

As discussed in the previous section, a newly un-live zombie is at its absolute peak of activity. It is engaged in an attempt to secure its own survival. This means finding sustenance, which in the case of zombies, means living human tissue (contrary to some reports, zombies do not have a fondness for baked goods). To a zombie, any presence of a potential victim is a complete distraction… one they cannot fail to pursue. This is why zombism spreads so rampantly at the scene of an initial outbreak. Once a victim becomes immobile, even though they may be a viable meal, they will be abandoned in favor of pursuit of another active victim.

In turn, these abandoned kills will rapidly rise as additional and new zombies. Once the zombie numbers become a horde, their own frantic activity and movement will distract them, causing them to kill and abandon more victims, creating more and more zombies. In this way, the tendency of zombies to function unthinkingly as a horde is actually a detriment to an individual zombie's un-life expectancy.

Zombies can and will extend their un-life expectancy by feeding on living human tissue, a particularly gruesome process, involving a gorge and purge cycle of consumption (think bulimia on steroids). Feeding will seldom take place until the zombies have eliminated all distractions of potential pursuit, so it is usually the final victims of a zombie killing spree who are actually consumed. Zombies lack any intelligence or memory, so they will not backtrack into their own killing fields, unless drawn there by sounds and movement of still-living victims. More likely than not, any still living wounded will become the first meals of new zombies arising from these same killing fields.

Stage one, feeding zombie.

Successful feeding will abate a zombie's deterioration for a matter of four to six hours; again this will depend on the rate of activity and other factors. Eventually, once all food sources have been consumed, the zombie is subject once again to the natural rates of decay, modified somewhat by the chemistry of the ZTA.

To break it down simply, in its first stage, a newly un-live zombie has an effective twenty-four to seventy-two hour window of opportunity. Any successful feeding within that window will sustain the zombie for four to six hours. Assuming, for instance, that the average zombie is able to feed successfully six times at about even intervals, they may increase their maximum motility potential from seventy-two, to one hundred and eight hours, roughly four and a half days. Thereafter, the zombie's ability to control and move their un-living body will begin to decrease rapidly. Any feeding that occurs abates the deterioration for a time, but

it must be remembered that, at no time, is the zombie capable in any way of reversing the effects of deterioration. Once the zombie passes its initial stage, it is a matter of roughly thirty-six hours before the zombie is reduced to lumbering, slow, methodical movements, with only short spurts of labored, more energetic movement in response to the presence of potential victims.

A zombie at this second stage plateaus and can sustain this reduced level of activity without feeding for a matter of months, possibly up to a year, depending largely on environmental and other degenerative factors.

One of the most persistent natural catalysts of tissue breakdown is the infestation of dead tissue by maggots (that's the larval stage of flies to you crosshair candidates). These insatiable eating machines can strip dead flesh from a carcass in a matter of weeks. Unfortunately, the zombification of human tissue by the ZTA acts as a repellent to flies (and virtually all other insects for that matter), and so this natural facilitator of decay is not a factor in zombie deterioration. However, zombies are subject to any number of bacterial, fungal, and mold infestations, which will not only make the zombies smell horrible and look gruesome, but will also hasten microcellular breakdown, eventually bringing about the zombies re-death by natural means.

Temperature and humidity can have a profound affect on both zombie motility and decay. Since zombies no longer breathe or have an operational circulatory system, they have become functionally cold-blooded. Therefore, logically, warmer temperatures will allow for greater ease of zombie movement. However, warmer temperatures will also promote increased growth of tissue necrotizing infestations, hastening the zombie's eventual re-demise. Various climatological conditions will have differing effects. See Table 1 for a summary of the effects of climactic conditions on zombie un-life expectancy.

TABLE 1: THE EFFECTS OF CLIMACTIC CONDITIONS ON ZOMBIE UN-LIFE EXPECTANCY

Humidity / Temp.	DRY	DRY/WET Seasonal	WET
HOT *Tropical and sub-tropical zones. Roughly from the Equator to about the 25th parallels North and South.*	**Tropical desert** Zombies exposed to these conditions will have an in initially increased motility due to the warm temperatures. The heat will sap body fluids through evaporation and dry out the corpse, decreasing effective un-life expectancy. Mold and fungus will be less of a factor; however, the dryness will severely shorten the second stage un-life expectancy. The zombie will dry out, becoming mummified within about four months, losing all mobility. **Note:** under these conditions, deep brain tissues can remain for several years that may be capable of harboring and transmitting the ZTA. **Un-life expectancy:** Four to seven months.	**Tropical savannah** In such conditions as this, zombies will retain a decent level of mobility due to warm temperatures. During the longer dryer season, mold and fungal infestations will occur but are likely to be minimal and progress more slowly. During the wet season, detrimental infestations will spike, becoming highly active. **Un-life expectancy:** Eight to ten months.	**Tropical forest** Wet tropical regions are the second re-deadliest regions for zombie un-life expectancy. Zombies here will have good motility but their rate of decay will be at its absolute highest. Mold, fungal, and bacterial infestations will be rampant and aggressive, causing the zombie to literally fall apart as water soaked tissues slough off. **Un-life expectancy:** Two to four months.
Warm w/seasonal variance *Roughly the 25th through the 35th parallels North and South.*	**Middle latitude desert** During the summer months, this region will have the same effects as tropical desert on zombies. During the winter months, zombies in this region will have increased daytime mobility and dry at a slower rate. Mold, bacterial, and fungal infestations will remain less likely and/or progress at a slower growth rate. **Un-life expectancy:** Five to eight months.	**Middle latitude temperate** This region is the most conducive to zombie existence, the average warm temperatures promote a high level of motility, and while mold, fungal, and bacterial infestations will be common, they will not be highly aggressive. Unfortunately, the vast majority of humans world wide, also choose to live in such regions. **Un-life expectancy:** Ten to twelve months.	**Middle latitude swamps and wetlands** While humans can live quite successfully in these regions, zombies will generally not fair so well. The terrain is usually difficult for foot travel. While motility may be high, so will mold, fungal, and bacterial infestations. **Un-life expectancy:** Six to eight months.
Cool w/seasonal variance *Roughly the 35th to the 72nd parallels North and South.*	**High latitude desert** In such a region of primarily cool desert, zombies will be slowed by the temperatures, and will freeze if the temperature reaches and remains at below freezing consistently for about eight hours. This is a distinct possibility about half of the year. There will be very little danger of mold or fungal infestations **Un-life expectancy:** Six to eight months.	**High latitude temperate** These regions will generally be good for zombies during the spring, summer, and fall seasons. Temperatures will be very reasonable and infestations non-aggressive. However, the harder winters of this region will easily re-kill zombies with below freezing temps. **Un-life expectancy:** seven to eight months.	**High latitude swamps and wetlands** This region will be difficult for zombies as there are many pitfalls to foot travel. As with all high latitude regions, freezing temperatures will be likely a good four months of every year and infestations will be common and aggressive in the wet weather the rest of the year. **Un-life expectancy:** four to eight months.
Cold *Roughly from the 72nd parallels North and South to the poles.*	**Arctic and Antarctic regions** Zombies in this region will freeze solid in a matter of hours after rising into un-life. Freezing ruptures cellular integrity and causes the re-death of the host body. There is the possibility, though slight, that deep tissue, due to ZTA chemistry, may survive being frozen and so retain the ability to harbor the ZTA and ultimately transfer it upon thawing. **Un-life expectancy:** Two to five hours.	**Arctic Tundra** This region is almost identical in effect to Arctic and Antarctic regions. There is the exception of a very brief (one month) pseudo-summer period of limited viability. See, Arctic and Antarctic regions. **Un-life expectancy:** Two to five hours.	**Arctic and Antarctic seashore** See, Arctic and Antarctic regions. **Un-life expectancy:** Two to five hours.

ZOMBIE PERCEPTION: SENSE AND SENSITIVITY

As with any animate creature, living or un-living, a zombie is hard wired for survival. To achieve this means one thing – consuming as much human flesh as possible, as often as possible. Zombies are always on the hunt.

As you do not want to become prey (you wouldn't have bought this book otherwise), it is important that you understand how a zombie hunts. To do that you need to understand a bit about zombie perception. And we don't mean perception as an intellectual exercise; we are strictly talking about what senses zombies have at their command to hunt with.

As has been covered already, zombies have a first stage window of opportunity that lasts about seventy-two hours and that feeding can extend this window. Zombies in this first stage are at their most dangerous, not only because they can move quickly and accurately, but also because they are at their most aggressive and at their height of perception.

Barring injury to the sense organs, first-stage zombies have all the senses of the human host. Having said this, there are a couple of exceptions. First, tactile stimulus (that would be touch to you crosshair candidates), including the perception of pain, is all but gone in a matter of minutes within the newly un-live zom. The ZTA must take over the nervous system simply to promote any motor function at all. It retains primary command pathways so that the body can be controlled, but most receptor information is rejected by the ZTA-controlled brain. Touch is reduced to a sense of pressure, pain is eliminated, and along the way, some of the finer

Zombies feel no pain and can withstand massive body damage.

motor skills and the most common of unconscious actions are eliminated (you won't see any zoms threading needles). Breathing and a heartbeat are examples of unconscious muscle actions that have ceased. Another is blinking. This will come into play during the discussion of zombie sight.

Smell is the second exception to the full range of human senses in the un-live. Remember, and we cannot say this too often, zombies are dead. They no longer breathe and this hampers the sense of smell. It's not entirely gone, but the fact that nothing is happening to draw air across the olfactory epithelium (look it up) makes it significantly less effective. Zombies may pick up on smells if they happen to move into an area where the air is permeated with one thing or another, but more likely they are stuck with the sense of the last thing they smelled prior to un-life (one can only hope that it was something particularly unpleasant).

Zombies have little or no sense of smell.

This leaves three remaining senses at the zombie's command: taste, sight, and hearing. Taken in order, taste is a sensation deeply connected to the sense of smell, so it is easy to imagine that the sense of taste is quite diminished. However, as zombies are intensely focused on feeding from one food source (that's you remember!), it's also safe to assume that they do crave and find the taste of that food source particularly satisfying. Despite this, the sense of taste plays no significant role in zombie hunting.

Zombie vision (and no we're not talking about a twenty-four hour zombie movie channel) plays a huge role in the zombie's early success but, like zombie movement, is seriously diminished over time. As mentioned previously, zombies no longer blink and this alone leads to the rapid deterioration of visual perception. Very quickly, their eyes will dry, creating a light film over the ocular surface. This film alone will occlude a zombie's vision considerably, reducing visual acuity to an unfocused blur of shapes in space. Depending on ambient humidity, this may occur in as little as four or five hours.

Along with drying out due to the failure to blink, a zombie's eyes are also subject to the accumulation of particulate matter, fungus, and mold spores, leading to further visual degradation. The very unlucky

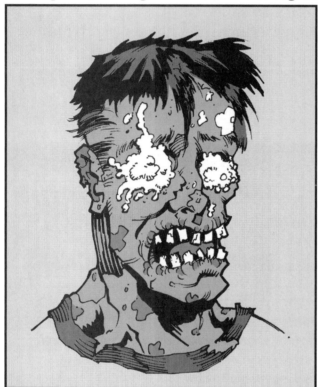

Zombies are prone to ocular fungal infections.

zombie may contract a severe fungal infection in its eyes and totally lose its vision within a few days, as a thick blanket of fungus covers its eyes. Regardless of the specific cause, the vast majority of zombies experience a rapid loss of eyesight. By the end of the first stage, it is unlikely that a zombie has any visual perception remaining beyond rough shapes and colors in a foggy field of view.

By the end of a couple of weeks, virtually one hundred percent of zombies will have experienced a loss of vision, reducing their perception to changes of light and dark, with some possible blotches of color. After a couple of months, zombies will be functionally blind, being able to see only a haze of light or total darkness. At this point, only bright flashes of light will attract their notice. Eventually, barring extremely unusual occurrences (say a scuba diver zom that somehow never lost its diving mask), zombies will become totally blind. This, however, will not stop them from their relentless pursuit of still-living flesh.

This brings us to sound. This is the one sense that zombies truly do possess. Unless a zombie's hearing is somehow obstructed (this can occur in many ways), their auditory perception actually becomes more acute. It is said that in a normal living human, when one sense is removed, the others grow stronger to compensate. In a zombie, this seems to be a function of the ZTA. While all of the other senses are diminished by design or natural development, a zombie's hearing seems to improve. Or… maybe it is in large part, simply the fact that the ambient sound level, which is a normal consequence of human activity, is all but removed.

Aside from their footfalls, bumping into things, and perhaps knocking over the occasional object, zombies themselves make no noise. Okay, we hear some of you out there saying, "But in the movies…" In response, we can say only one thing, (sigh) "crosshairs."

Remember, movies are made to entertain you. During the zombie apocalypse, the zoms will be trying to eat you. While on the wide-screen a moaning, even speaking ("braaaaiiiinnnss") zom may add dramatic effect, let us remind you (once again) that zoms are dead; they do not breathe and no breathing means no vocalization. Think about it for a minute and you will realize they're actually a damn sight scarier that way. And, we assure you the zombie apocalypse will be scary.

It may simply be that because the workings of the ear are actually internal, they are far less susceptible to the factors that will diminish the zom's other senses. In any case, sound is the zom's primary sensory tool. It's what attracts them and what they follow in pursuit of prey, particularly once their vision is all but gone.

Common ear obstructions.

The first-stage zombie relies heavily on sound as an attractor and means of locating prey. In a world gone silent, sounds of human activity will be very easily distinguishable. The second-stage zombie hunts almost exclusively by sound, and while it can no longer hunt as actively as it did during its first stage, the fact that it is almost entirely silent can sometimes give it the element of surprise.

Armed with this knowledge, you will hopefully understand the importance of (particularly during the first weeks of the zombie apocalypse) staying in one secure place and keeping as quiet as possible.

Just remember, zombies want to eat you. It isn't personal, for the zombies it's the natural order of things. This is not to say that you should be in any way sympathetic to the zombie's un-live circumstances. For you save the whales types who just think that the zombies should be left alone to pursue their nature within their own special habitat, feel free to step out and offer to feed them.

Zoms are relentless in their pursuit; they will keep coming. So remember… they may not be able to feel you, smell you, or even, after a time, see you, but they can hear you, and you do taste good to them.

Purina doesn't really make Zombie Chow.

ZOMBIE INTERACTION: OOPS, PARDON ME

The short version here is simply, they don't interact. It may seem that they do, particularly in a horde, but in actuality, each zom is acting solely for its own benefit. The truth is, in a horde situation, the zoms are in competition with one another, each trying to be the first to get each fresh victim.

There is no attempt between zombies to communicate or act cooperatively in any manner. If zombies share a goal and act in some appearance of unity, it is purely an illusion of circumstance. Zombies may be attracted to any sound, even sounds made inadvertently by other zombies, which accounts for why they so often appear in large numbers. What they seek is a live victim whom they can identify easily from the sound of breathing and presumably, when in close enough proximity, even a heartbeat. As zombies clearly lack these key indicators, they can be differentiated from prey and will be ignored.

Zombies do not cooperate with each other.

Late-stage zombies will spend a great deal of their existence bumping into things, even each other, without so much as a "pardon me." Until something attracts their attention, zombies simply continue in whatever direction they happen to be headed until they bump into something or some new distraction pulls them to a new course.

ZOMBIE SUPREMACY: A NUMBERS GAME

When the apocalypse hits, the ZTA will spread with amazing speed. This will be due largely to the fact that humans have a tendency toward ignorance, and at heart, have a rather compassionate attitude regarding the ill and infirm. Hospitals will be the worst possible places to be

during an outbreak. In their ingrained training to treat this condition as a normal disease, doctors and nurses will make repeated attempts to treat and understand. In the process, they will be among the first to be victims of the ZTA. Hospitals and clinics will be instant breeding grounds and will fuel the unchecked spread of zombism. As it expands to the streets, people will stand in disbelief, watching in horror, unwittingly allowing themselves to become zombie chow.

People will run and they will hide, but without the benefit of understanding (which is why you bought this book), they will make bad choices, leaving them open to being found and or overrun. They will venture out into relative silence looking for help, unaware of the potential danger and the widespread nature of the crisis… and they will become zombie chow (or zombies themselves).

In very short order, the ZTA will have transformed the majority of the human race. It is exponential, each new zom turns two or three people, and those new zoms turn two or three people, and pretty soon, there are far more zoms than living humans. (It's a little like joining Amway, only without the tapes and seminars.) The zoms will be supreme rulers of the Earth, having taken down the one species most successful at carving its own existence from the planet upon which it lives. The biggest problem, of course, is that the zoms will not even know it!

ZOMBIE PERPETUATION: A MODEL FOR EXTINCTION

Zombies do not reproduce, the only means of perpetuation they have at their disposal is to transform living humans into additional zombies...

and they do with great rapidity due to their lack of any thought regarding the process. Very soon, they have simply exchanged their only food source for more zombies. Their pursuit of additional food will send them off randomly in whatever direction they happen to be facing in search of more living humans. Within months of the beginning of the zombie apocalypse, the zombies will have sealed their fate of eventual extinction. Even should they manage to somehow discover (purely by random chance) camps of living humans, and should they be able to overrun these encampments, they are only beginning the cycle of un-life that can only lead eventually to re-death.

The ZTA can really only be described as a plague of Biblical proportion. In writing this manual, our job is simply to see that there remain a few Noahs. The zombie apocalypse is indeed survivable, and it is our sincere hope to ensure that enough of you survive to allow the human race to return to its rightful place at the pinnacle of the Earth's species, perhaps a bit smarter for the effort.

ZOMBOLOGY: COMMON SENSE

Hopefully, we have now provided you with enough knowledge about zombies that you will understand and never underestimate the threat at hand. Zombies are not complicated creatures; in actuality, they are extremely simple. Your job is to avoid them. Recognizing that this is not going to be completely possible, in future chapters we lay out how to prepare for these encounters and what to do when they do happen. If there is any essential wisdom to be imparted, it is – never get sentimental about a zombie as it is following its natural programming and will not hesitate to make a meal of you. So, no matter the circumstance or appearances, you should never hesitate to re-kill a zombie with all haste. Future chapters, of course, will cover weapons and re-killing methods.

CHAPTER 2: THE PLAN

The ultimate plan is simple survival, but there is more to consider.
Where are you going to go? How are you going to get there? What will
be needed for survival besides a secure place to hang your hat?

By purchasing this book, you've proven yourself to be far ahead of the
curve. You've done what the vast majority of people lack the courage to
do. You've acknowledged the coming zombie apocalypse. It's now time to
build on that knowledge.

The key to winning any battle is planning (don't kid yourself: this is a
battle; indeed, it's a war for survival). A successful battle plan has two
basic components: Strategy (what you want to accomplish) and tactics
(how you're going to accomplish it). In this chapter, we'll concentrate
primarily on strategy. Specific tactics will be covered in chapters 3, 4, 5,
7, 8, 9, 10 (in fact, most of the rest of this book).

When developing your overall strategy, you must keep in mind that the
rise of the zombies can happen at any time (probably when it's least
convenient), so start now and avoid the Christmas rush (so to speak!).
Your plan should be based around the time line found in chapter 10 and
contain the following elements:

1) An ultimate destination. A single family home or apartment is not the most defendable location. You'll want to establish a more secure base as soon as is feasible (we'll discuss the best possible destinations later).
2) Map out multiple routes from your starting point to the site of your chosen stronghold. The zombies will be everywhere, so be prepared to improvise.
3) In the short term, you'll need to zombie-proof your current home as much as you can. Be prepared to stay put for at least a month. Make sure you have food, water, etc., for that long.
4) Chances are you'll be at work or school (or whatever it is that you do to occupy your time) when the zombies rise. Make sure you use the resulting chaos to your advantage in order to reach home safely.
5) If you're going to work with a group to survive the apocalypse, be sure to stay in contact. Work out your meeting places and delegate chores. Redundancy is highly recommended. That way, if one of your group is killed (or zombified), someone else can pick up the slack.

If you're in a group, keep in mind that there can be only one leader. Democracy is a wonderful thing, but the zombie apocalypse is not the time or place for a debate. If you're not in charge, but are the type who wants to argue every order and decision, see Appendix E.

It has been suggested that the best places to go during the zombie apocalypse are a desert island, off-shore oil rig, or an Arctic (or Antarctic) research base. These all have the advantages of isolation and inaccessibility. Plus, it will be virtually impossible for the zombies to catch you unawares. However, the very features, which make these

If you can't get there easily, and can't re-supply once you're there... crosshairs.

locations so attractive, render them impractical for most people to get to. Your goals must be realistic.

When choosing a base, fortress, or stronghold (or whatever you want to call it), remember that you're going to be there for at least a year, so you'll want to consider the following questions:

1) What is the structure made from? Is it sturdy enough to keep the zombies out?
2) Does it have multiple entrances/exits? How easy will it be to secure these against intrusion?
3) How many windows does the building have? (Lots of windows, especially pane glass, is bad.) How will you board them up?
4) Does it have its own power source? (That's a generator for you crosshair candidates.)
5) Does it have cooking and sanitary facilities?
6) What are its storage capabilities (both cold and dry)?

Based on these criteria, we have concluded that your best options are either a national (or state) park ranger station or a warehouse club store (if you live in a coastal area, a lighthouse could also be a good choice).

Holing up at a lighthouse just may present an entirely different set of problems.

A ranger station (or lighthouse) offers sturdy construction (usually brick or cinder block), a remote location, a low human (and, therefore, low zombie) population density, its own generator, and emergency supplies. Plus, since they're generally built in large clearings, you'll have a three-hundred-sixty degree view, making it difficult for the zombies to sneak up on you. The drawbacks are: the on-site supplies are limited so you'll need to bring a lot with you and you'll have to drive through miles of zombie infested countryside to get there. Note: Ranger stations are not to be confused with fire watchtowers. These are to be avoided. The last thing you want is to be trapped three stories in the air with the only stairs down filled with zombies.

Fire watchtowers are not a good idea.

The warehouse club store may be your best choice. They're built with cinderblock and cement, have almost no windows, only one vulnerable entrance (the front door), and almost everything you'll need is already on hand in quantities that will last for months (this includes food, water, first aid supplies, tools, generators, fuel, and even clothing). If you can find one that shares a common wall with a home improvement store, you're golden! Just break through the wall and you'll have almost everything you'll need. The only downside is, that being so close to a population center means you'll have a lot more zombie neighbors (they don't make a lot of noise, but they're always trying to put the bite on you).

Wearhouse centers may just be your all-in-one survival locations.

There are those of you who are asking, "Why go to all the trouble and hazard to move? Why not just fortify your house ala Robert Neville (from Matheson's 'I Am Legend' for you crosshair candidates)?" Well, Neville died at the end of that book and all three versions of the movie. So, obviously his is not your best plan. Furthermore, if you think you know better than we do, why didn't you write this book? (We direct you to Appendix E).

PLANNING/PREPARATION CHECKLIST

1) *Watch the news and internet for any signs of ZTA outbreak.* ❑

2) *Zombie-proof your current home.* ❑

3) *Map out your Day Zero route(s) from work to home.* ❑

4) *Gather your weapons and supplies.* ❑

5) *Familiarize yourself with your chosen weapons.* ❑

6) *Zombie-proof your car.* ❑

7) *Choose your long-term base.* ❑

8) *Assess the structure for weaknesses.* ❑

9) *Map out multiple routes from your home to your chosen base.* ❑

10) *Mark locations of potential supply points near your chosen base.* ❑
(Stockyards, dairy farms, refineries, construction companies, etc.)

11) *Install your in-home generator in preparation for the failure of the power grid.* ❑

12) *Install your ham radio set-up.* ❑

13) *Assemble your zombie apocalypse study materials (see appendix D).* ❑

14) *Thoroughly study your zombie apocalypse texts and films.* ❑

15) *Select your survivor group.* ❑

16) *Schedule regular strategy meetings with your group members.* ❑

17) *Assign tasks to various group members, based on their strengths.* ❑

18) *Thouroughly plan and coordinate arrival at, and entry to your Chosen base, calculating travel times of group members.* ❑

19) *Conduct zombie apocalypse practice drills as needed.* ❑

20) *Prepare zombie lures for instant deployment.* ❑

21) *Review the manual and re-check all your planning and supplies* ❑

22) *Practice your shovel blade cooking.* ❑

23) *Relax and laugh at all the pathetic crosshair candidates that are on the verge of becoming zombie chow.* ❑

CHAPTER 3: PREPARATION

Preparation is a major part of planning. It doesn't matter how good your plan is if you're not ready to implement it at a moment's notice.

Your first step should be to scout out the location of your stronghold. Make a thorough study of the building. Examine the doors and windows with an eye toward how you're going to zombie-proof them. One thing, though, try to be subtle about it. You don't want the current occupants to think you're casing the place in order to rob it. Winding up in jail on suspicion of robbery charges will be detrimental to your chances of survival once the zombies rise.

Don't get caught casing your future stronghold.

Secondly, you'll want to start gathering your supplies (a comprehensive list will be found in the next chapter). Most likely, you'll need to do this a little at a time, since most people lack the financial resources to buy a year's worth of stuff all at once (remember that the zombie apocalypse can happen at any time, so don't wait too long to get started).

Third, get your vehicle ready (see chapter 5). Ideally, your post-apocalypse vehicle should be loaded, zombie-proofed, and stored in your locked garage until you're ready to move. However, we realize that there may be people out there without the capital to do  this. If you need to use your car every day (for work or whatever), our recommendation is that you zombie-proof it anyway. Sure, people will laugh at you, but remember, they laughed at Noah, too. Besides, once they're all zombies (or zombie chow), you'll have the last laugh.

Fourth, stock up on detailed paper maps of all the areas you expect to travel through. Remember, once the zombies rise, there will be no internet or GPS. Make sure you understand how to read a map and compass. These are not difficult skills to acquire (unless you're a complete crosshair candidate). Note: telephone service (both cell and landline) will be unavailable, so you'll need an alternative form of communication (Ham or CB radios are your best bet).

Fifth, assemble your cache of weapons (see chapter 7 for your best options). Be sure to obey all your local gun laws. As previously stated, you don't want to be in jail when the apocalypse hits.

Sixth, you'll want to zombie-proof your existing dwelling. This will consist primarily of boarding up the windows and installing heavy crossbars on the outer doors. Your best choice for the windows is to use three-quarter inch plywood (no cheap particleboard) and countersunk deck screws. You'll need to measure all the windows and cut the plywood to size. Installing the boards on the inside will be easiest (okay, so the zombies will be able to break the glass, but as long as they can't get in, who cares?).

Do your best to zombie-proof your dwelling... before the zoms rise.

If you don't have central heating/air conditioning in your home, make sure that you have window air conditioning units in place. Cut your plywood to accommodate the units. This is important because, once your house is boarded up, ventilation will be minimal. If you live in a two-story house, figure on boarding up the second floor windows anyway. The zombies probably won't be able to get to them, but why take chances. It's not a bad idea to cut peep holes in the boards so you can keep the zombies under surveillance (closed-circuit TV cameras mounted at strategic points on the house would be better).

Make sure that you have a generator connected to the house's main junction box so you can switch over at a moment's notice. The city power grid probably won't fail completely for a couple of months, but better safe than sorry. Remember though, using a generator will make noise and therefore could attract zoms, so a choice will have to be made. Use your best judgement depending on your particular situation.

Keep track of what is going on around you.

If you're part of a group of survivors, it might be a good idea to gather everyone at one house. That way you can all pool your resources and you'll only need to zombie-proof one place. Plus, it'll be a lot less hazardous if you don't need to gather your group after the zombies rise.

Once the zombies do rise, it's vital you stay indoors and keep as quiet as possible. Zombies hunt primarily by sound, so draw as little attention to yourself as possible. Be prepared to stay put for about a month. Civilization will have almost entirely collapsed by then and it'll be pretty much just you and the zoms.

The last step in your preparations will be planning entry to your long-term base and zombie-proofing it. This, of course, will be complicated by the presence of the zoms. But a little level-headed clear thinking goes a long way. You're not going to want to fight your way through a horde of zoms once you reach your stronghold, so what's the alternative? You need to lure them away. The best way to do this is by using portable CD players (boom boxes) (We can see some of you out there scratching your heads and saying "huh?"). Keeping in mind that zombies hunt primarily by sound, a musical lure is obvious. We recommend using music with a heavy backbeat (Michael Jackson's "Thriller" comes to mind), since the heavy bass will attract the zoms most efficiently. Just place the boom box on the street about a mile from your base, put it on continuous

repeat, crank up the volume, and drive off (it's vital that you make sure that the batteries are fresh). The sound will attract most, if not all the zoms in the area. Find a secure spot to wait (at least twenty minutes), then proceed to your base. Make sure that you stay quiet while you're waiting or the zoms will find you.

Once you reach your base, you'll need to clear the area of any remaining zoms, gain entry, make sure it's clear, get everyone inside, and secure the entrance. Since the vast majority of the zoms you'll be dealing with will most likely be stage two, you should have about twenty to thirty minutes to accomplish these tasks (plenty of time). You should be able to re-kill any zoms outside the building without even leaving your vehicles as you drive up to the target entrance. Once you've reached your target, presumably the front door, you'll probably need to break in. Simply smash the glass with a crowbar, tire iron, or shovel to gain entry (yeah, you could shoot out the glass, but why waste ammo?). Once you've gained entry, immediately dispatch a search-and-destroy team to clear the building of any zoms.

Once the building has been cleared, you can secure the entrance. If you've chosen a warehouse club store as your stronghold (our recommendation), you'll find plenty of materials inside to secure the entrance (check the home improvement section as garage door

Get in quickly and clear the structure.

segments are probably your best bet). As part of your team secures the front door, send another to open the garage door on the auto repair shop. Then, you just drive your vehicles inside, drop, and lock the door, and you're safe and sound and can begin setting up housekeeping. We realize that this sounds like a lot to do in a short period of time, but we believe that it can be done. If you're that concerned about the timing, it might be a good idea to get your group together and conduct some practice drills at a paintball arena or some other large venue.

Once you're safe and secure inside your newly acquired base, there are just a few things left to do. None of them are terribly complicated and you can take care of them more-or-less at your leisure.

1) Connect a generator to the building's junction box and get the lights and air conditioning operating.
2) Take a detailed inventory of all food, water, and other supplies and materials on hand.

3) Find the roof access so you can set up observation posts to keep the zombies under surveillance.

4) Section a part of the building off to serve as living quarters. The office area is probably your best choice, since it's already partitioned.

5) By this point, your group will probably be hungry, so preparing a meal wouldn't be a bad idea. We recommend making it as lavish an affair as possible. After all, you've just cleared a major hurdle in your quest for survival, so a celebration is in order.

Assign these tasks based on your group member's strengths and skills. Everyone should be aware of their jobs before you even set foot in your new home. As previously stated, planning and preparation go hand-in-hand and are vital to your survival.

We realize that it's impossible to completely crosshair-proof your plans, because there's always unforeseen factors. However, meticulous preparation can and will minimize the risks. Remember, all it takes is one catastrophic crosshair moment to make the most level-headed survivor zombie chow. So, keep your wits about you and expect the unexpected.

The unexpected can and will happen, so preparation is essential.

ZOMBIE APOCALYPSE SHOPPING LIST.

1) *Canned & dried food and MREs (one month supply).* ☐

2) *Bottled water.* ☐

3) *Weapons and ammunition.* ☐

4) *¾ inch plywood and hardware.* ☐

5) *Durable clothes and boots.* ☐

6) *Toothbrushes, toothpaste and dental floss.* ☐

7) *Personal hygiene products.* ☐

8) *Toilet paper.* ☐

9) *More weapons and ammunition.* ☐

10) *Medical supplies.* ☐

11) *Flashlights and lanterns.* ☐

12) *A good tool kit.* ☐

13) *A SHOVEL!* ☐

14) *An SUV.* ☐

15) *Chain-link fencing.* ☐

16) *A snowplow for the SUV.* ☐

17) *A compass and maps.* ☐

18) *Gasoline and diesel fuel.* ☐

19) *A generator.* ☐

20) *Even more weapons and ammunition.* ☐

21) *Ham radio equipment, base, mobile and hand-held.* ☐

22) *Boom boxes w/plenty of batteries & CDs (zombie lures).* ☐

23) *Books, playing cards & board games (quiet entertainment).* ☐

24) *Duct tape.* ☐

25) *Just in case we forgot to mention it, plenty of weapons and ammunition.* ☐

CHAPTER 4: SUPPLIES

What do you really need and how will you actually get it?

Weapons are the most obvious things you'll need (so obvious in fact, that we've devoted an entire chapter to them). But, there are plenty of other things required for survival that you'll need to assemble before the zombies rise. We'll discuss them in order of priority.

FOOD AND WATER:

Avoiding becoming a meal for zombies is pointless if you wind up starving to death yourself. Therefore, a sufficient supply of food is a must. You'll want to stock primarily non-perishable foodstuffs. Canned or dried foods are your best bet. MREs (Meals Ready to Eat – military rations) are also an excellent option (especially if

Military style "field meals" are good for a short haul.

you're not much of a cook). These are all readily available (most outdoor outfitters carry MREs) in large quantities.

Water will not be as much of a problem as you might think. Within six months of industry shutting down, practically all water (even rainwater) will be safe to drink. Meanwhile, bottled water is available by the case virtually everywhere. Other options include boiled tap water (boiling the water for fifteen minutes will destroy any harmful microorganisms) or water purification tablets. These can be found at most outdoor outfitters (pick up some while you're buying your MREs).

Water will be easy to obtain.

Inasmuch as you're going to be living in your stronghold for a year, eventually you're going to want some creature comforts, such as running water. In that case, you'll need to dig a well. The major problem will be where to drill. You'll need to avoid gas lines, electrical conduits, storm drains, sewers, and of course, the now defunct city water lines. The plans and charts showing the location of all of these are available at your local public works office. See Appendix D for recommended texts on drilling wells and installing water pumps.

MEDICAL SUPPLIES:

Most people lack any formal medical training, so you'll want to concentrate on first-aid type supplies, such as bandages, antibiotic ointments, and pain killers. As you're assembling your supplies, you'll

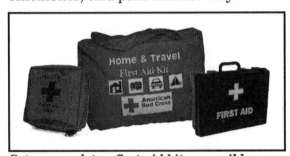

Get as complete a first aid kit as possible.

be limited to over-the-counter meds (ibuprofen and the like). However, once civilization collapses, more sophisticated drugs will be available at hospitals, pharmacies, and medical supply outlets. It is also advisable to include things like suture kits and wound cauterizers (available at any drug or medical supply store) among your supplies.

It is highly recommended that you take at least one first-aid course before the rise of the zombies (afterwards, it'll be too late). Remember that there will be no clinics or emergency rooms during (or after) the zombie apocalypse and doctors will be few and far between (kind of like government run healthcare, but without the lines). Related to this, make sure you include oral hygiene supplies like toothpaste, toothbrushes, and dental floss (if you don't generally floss, it might be a good idea to start). After all, there won't be any dentists around either.

HEAT AND LIGHT:

As previously discussed, you'll want to have at least one generator… two would be better (it never hurts to have a back up). Space heaters are also recommended (it beats freezing in the winter). Flashlights or lanterns are vital. Make sure you include a large supply of batteries and/or fuel for these things. In addition, it's advisable to include flexible photovoltaic panels and a current inverter in your gear. These will enable you to keep your rechargeable batteries powered up with out excess strain on your generator. The power grid will eventually fail (this includes electricity, communications, gas, and water/sewerage), so you must anticipate this.

There are many types of generators available

Most of the things on this list will be yours for the taking once civilization collapses, but to limit your contact with the zombies, you'll want to keep post-apocalyptic foraging to a minimum. We cannot stress enough the need to plan ahead.

TOOLS:

A comprehensive tool kit is extremely important. Your vehicle(s) or other equipment could break down at any time and an immediate replacement may not be readily available. Therefore, it's vital that you're able to keep it operational until a replacement can be obtained. Your kit should include a hammer, multiple screwdrivers (both standard and cross-point) of various sizes, a good ratchet set (SAE and Metric), a power drill with multiple bits and batteries, a power circular saw (battery powered), a hand saw, a hacksaw, assorted wrenches, a crowbar, a pair of bolt cutters, and a shovel (that's right, a shovel). A good military style collapsible shovel can be obtained at most camping/outdoor stores. On the other hand, a good ten-inch steel shovel is very easily obtained and though a bit harder to carry, makes an excellent shovel choice. Note: It never hurts to have a plan "B". It's possible that some of your tools may get lost or damaged. In that case, you'll want to be on the lookout for a Mac, Snap-on, or Matco truck. These vehicles are rolling tool stores, so you'll likely find anything you might need.

A shovel is probably the most useful thing a zombie apocalypse survivor can carry. Its possible uses are endless. You can pry open crates with it. You can use it as a wedge to barricade a door. You can re-kill zombies with it. You can use it as a makeshift mess kit for cooking over an open fire (see Appendix C). You can even dig a hole with it if you're so inclined. What's more, having a shovel will make you a legend amongst your fellow survivors. After all, anyone who can travel through miles of zombie infested countryside, battle the un-live, wild animals and marauders, face terrors unimagined in the pre-apocalypse world, and still manage to hang on to his shovel is clearly a force to be reckoned with.

When selecting your tools, look for the highest quality (not necessarily the most expensive). In preparing for the zombie apocalypse, you don't

Pre-cased tools sets can be very convenient, and are available in a wide variety.

want to do things on the cheap. Your survival is at stake, so money should be no object (to put it another way, the end of civilization as we know it is no time to pinch pennies).

CLOTHING:

Good quality, durable clothes and boots are highly recommended. You can dress however you wish (after all, who'll be around to make fun of you?), but we advise simplicity. Jeans and flannel shirts are always a good choice. So are military fatigues or hunting gear. All of these are sturdy, yet easy to move in. Calf length hiking boots are recommended for the ankle support that they offer (you don't want to wind up with a sprain at a critical moment). Don't forget good quality socks.

COMMUNICATIONS:

Radios are a "must"!

As stated in the previous chapter, phone service and the internet will not be available. Therefore, you'll need an alternative. We believe that your best options are either two-meter, amateur Ham or CB radios. The Ham radios should be your first choice since they tend to have stronger signals and are less subject to interference than CBs. Both are inexpensive and available at any electronics store. You'll want to include a base unit (at your stronghold), dashboard units for all of your vehicles, and personal walkie-talkies for everyone in your group. Be sure to decide on which frequencies/channels you're going to use ahead of time.

PERSONAL SURVIVAL KIT:

We highly recommended that you carry the following items on your person at all times:

1) A flashlight
2) A canteen of water
3) A walkie-talkie (if you're with a group)
4) A first-aid kit
5) Trail rations (protein bars or the like)
6) A fully loaded holdout gun (save the last round for yourself)

These items should be stored in a belt, fanny pack, or shoulder bag.

Be prepared.

If you become separated from your group and have to hide by yourself and await rescue, having this kit could make the difference between life and death (or un-life). As previously stated, being prepared is your best defense.

MISCELLANEOUS SUPPLIES:

There are other items you'll want to keep in mind. These are the sort of things you don't think about until you actually need them – like oil and other necessary fluids for your vehicle(s). A few cans of fix-a-flat are also a good idea in case of an emergency (trying to change a tire when the zombies are closing in is a bad move). Personal hygiene items like toilet paper should be included in your stock. Other useful items include: binoculars, a can opener (manual, of course), cooking and eating utensils, pots and pans, a camp stove, sleeping bags, a durable pair of leather work gloves, several feet of rope, towing chains, jerry cans (for carrying your fuel), a hand pump/siphon (for obtaining the fuel from gas stations. No electricity, remember?), a wind-proof cigarette lighter (before you say that you don't smoke, portable fire is always a handy item) and last but certainly not least don't forget a good supply of duct tape, its possible uses are endless.

Of course, you'll want some form of entertainment, particularly during the month you're holed up in your home. Make sure you stick to quiet forms of entertainment like books, cards, or board games (zombies hunt by sound, remember?) So, save the DVDs and video games until you're safe in your well-secured stronghold.

There's a lot of stuff that's easy to forget... Don't!

CHAPTER 5: TRAVEL AND TRANSPORTATION

As discussed in previous chapters, the collapse of civilization will occur with surprising rapidity. Within a month, you will be able to travel unchallenged (except by the zombies, of course). In this chapter, we'll cover how to get from point A to point B (or any other points, for that matter).

If you've been paying attention, you'll know that your vehicle should be ready to go before the apocalypse hits. You don't want to be wandering around on foot searching for something appropriate when the zombies are roaming the streets, looking for a meal.

When choosing a vehicle, consider fuel capacity, passenger/cargo space, speed, and overall ruggedness. Let's look at some of your vehicle choices, so you can pick one that will suit you best.

HELICOPTERS AND OTHER AIRCRAFT:

Since the vast majority of people are not pilots and once the zombies rise, you're not going to have time to learn to be one, this type of transport is unlikely to be of use to you. We mention them merely in the interests of thoroughness.

TANKS (YOU'RE WELCOME):

These offer phenomenal protection from the zombie hordes and will be virtually unstoppable. But (you knew there was a "but" coming), they're slow, hard to steer, have limited cargo and passenger space, and require frequent refueling. Remember, tanks are designed as combat machines, not transportation.

Believe it or not – not a good apocalypse vehicle.

SEMI-TRUCKS:

These have several advantages – they're big, fast, have a large fuel

capacity, and can carry a lot of cargo. However, driving a vehicle of this size does require a specialized skill set. Unless you can handle one competently, you probably should look for something smaller.

TRACTORS AND OTHER FARM OR CONSTRUCTION VEHICLES:

See tanks and semi-trucks.

SPORTS CARS:

These are not recommended because, despite their superior handling, they're road machines, built for speed and aesthetics. They'll be of little use if you have to go off-road or force your way through a zombie horde.

HYBRIDS AND SMART CARS:

This is the bloody zombie apocalypse! If you're going to worry about that environmentalist wacko, carbon footprint crapola under these circumstances, see Appendix E.

These are just a few examples. Ultimately, your best choice is a four-wheel-drive SUV. They're durable, reliable, have a large fuel capacity, and plenty of room for passengers and gear. Plus, in the event of inclement weather (i.e., snow) or the need to veer off-road, the 4WD will be a definite asset. 4WD pick-up trucks are good too, except for their open cargo beds. For those of you who need to include child safety seats, an SUV is really the only choice.

Choose something rugged and spacious.

You'll need to make some modifications to your truck. This should be done ahead of time. You'll need to add additional protection over the glass to keep the zombies from smashing their way in. You could bolt or weld sheet metal armor over the windows (don't forget to cut out viewing slits). It doesn't need to be particularly thick, just enough to keep the zombies out. The drawback to this is that it severely limits your field of vision. A better alternative is chain link fencing. It's light, easy to obtain and work with, and the visual obstruction will be minimal. Remember, all you need to do is keep the zombies out long enough for you to get away.

Adding a snowplow to your truck is highly advisable. In addition to it

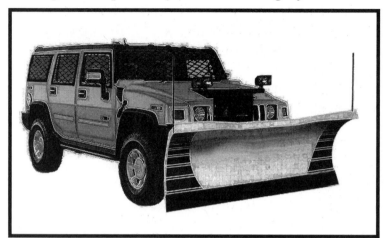

being very handy when driving through a zombie horde, you must remember that there will be no snow removal crews working during the zombie apocalypse (or after it for that matter), so you'll be on your own.

SOME ADDITIONAL VEHICLES:

Motorcycles will be handy getaway vehicles in a tight spot. So, if you don't know how to ride a motorcycle, it might be a good idea to learn. It's also a good idea to keep one or more bicycles in your gear. They're

Rugged hybrid bicycles, and enduro motorcycles are your best choices.

almost silent and, therefore, attract little zombie attention. This makes them excellent scout vehicles. Plus, they require no fuel (we know that bikes offer little in the way of protection, but all you really need is to be faster than the zombies – or at least your companions).

One guy asked about go-carts. Our response was: Are you serious! You might as well be riding a lawn tractor! If you think that these things are a viable choice, you're a crosshair candidate (see Appendix E).

KNOW WHERE YOU'RE GOING:

With your vehicle properly outfitted, you're now ready for travel. As

discussed in chapter 2, you should already have a destination in mind before setting out. Wandering aimlessly is just asking to become a drive-thru meal for zombies.

Daylight travel is advisable because, unlike the zoms you need to see. It will be much easier to avoid not only the zoms, but also other road hazards if you're not relying solely on your headlights. Bear in mind that zoms are relatively silent, so you're likely to see them before you hear them. Therefore, the chances of getting caught unawares by the zoms are much greater at night.

Zombies don't need light.

Avoid major population centers. There will be more zombies per square foot there than anywhere else. You'll also want to avoid the interstate system, because when the panicked mass evacuations occur, the main highways are the route everyone will use to leave the cities. Consequently, these will be jammed with the wreaked and abandoned cars left behind when

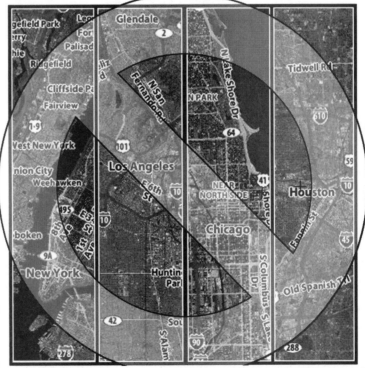

Avoid the downtown center of any major metropolitan area!

their occupants became zombie chow (or zombies themselves). State and county roads will probably be your best bet.

If your ultimate destination is more than a day's drive away, travel will pose some additional difficulties, but nothing insurmountable. Keep in mind that you'll need to find temporary lodging while in transit. There will be plenty of abandoned buildings to choose from. Your best options are places like fire or police stations or post offices (that's right, we said post offices). These are generally heavy brick or cinderblock structures with only a few windows and limited access (steel doors are fairly typical), so fortifying them will be a relatively simple matter. Many of them even have their own generators.

| *Police Stations* | *Fire Houses* | *Post Offices* |

In most towns these are good overnight accommodations. Safety before comfort anyway.

Another excellent feature of this type of building is that most of them have fenced-in parking lots. This is highly advantageous because it allows you to secure your vehicles for the night and not have to fight your way through zombies to get to them in the morning. This is a consideration because chances are you'll attract the attention of the local zombies while you're fortifying the building. You'll probably have to cut the lock off the gate and then re-secure it from the inside. Then in the morning, you just drive through the gate (yet another good reason to have a snowplow on your truck).

It is highly recommended that you stop at least two hours before sundown so you will have time to clear the building of any zombie

Good for moving more than snow!

infestation and then zombie-proof it. As always, once it's dark, keep your movements to a minimum and stay as quiet as possible (no sense in ringing the zombie dinner bell, as it were). It is vital that you remain aware of where the exits are on the off chance that the zombies breach your fortifications and threaten to overrun your group. Always keep your weapons handy and be prepared for a quick escape.

OTHER TRAVEL HAZARDS:

There are definite dangers to travelling in a post-apocalyptic, zombie-infested world (besides the zombies that is), so you need to be aware of them. Among these are other survivors (see chapter 6), wild animals, and domestic dogs gone feral. Of these, the feral dogs will most likely be the biggest hazard. Wild animals will tend to avoid humans even as nature begins to claim the urban areas.

You will be able to re-domesticate them later.

Dogs, on the other hand, are pack animals by nature, so when their human families (their packs) die out or become zombies, the dogs will seek out a substitute. This substitute, of course, will be other dogs. And while it's true that dogs prefer fresh meat, they have been known to eat carrion if nothing else is available. With the rise of the zombies, carrion will be abundant (food on the foot, so to speak).

You begin to see the problem. Wild dog packs will act in concert to bring down prey, and thanks to the presence of the zombies, they'll be accustomed to attacking human size targets, seeing them as an easy meal (after all, the zoms don't fight back). You must remain alert to this hazard at all times. Try to stay in open areas where the dogs can't box you in, keep your weapons handy at all times (always good advice), and when you see the dogs, don't be sentimental. These aren't cute little Spot or Rover or Fido from down the street, they are slavering beasts that will tear your throat out and eat you for lunch. Treat them like zombies and shoot!

There's just one last thing before moving on. There are those of you who are contemplating travel by water, sailing either across the lake or down river. This is not a good idea. In the first place, boats are almost impossible to zombie-proof. Second, there are only so many places you can go ashore (what if zoms are overrunning the dock, hmmm?).

Actually, zoms don't row either, but that doesn't remove the potential threat.

Furthermore, even if you can go ashore, you have no transportation (you hadn't thought of that, eh? That's why we're here). Finally, if the zombies manage to board your boat, you have nowhere to go (zombie horde + limited space + no escape route = zombie chow).

We can hear some smartass asking "How are the zombies gonna get on the boat? They don't swim." Well, they don't drown, either. (Look, do you want to survive the zombie apocalypse or not? If so, avoid boats, if not see Appendix E).

CHAPTER 6: COMPANIONS AND OTHER SURVIVORS

It's a fact that people will survive the initial outbreak despite not having read this book or being prepared as well as you are. By either aggressiveness, cunning, or sheer dumb luck, they'll have managed to somehow stay alive and one step ahead of the zombie hordes.

Inevitably, they're going to show up at your caravan or stronghold and want what you have. They will try to get it by trickery, theft, or simply by killing everyone in your party. As the leader of your group, you are faced with a difficult decision. What are you going to do about them? You have three options:

1) Give them what they want in hopes that they'll go away and leave you alone.
2) Fight it out. You worked hard to get this far and you're not going to let a bunch of slackers take advantage of you.
3) Let them join your group. Safety in numbers and all that.

Taking each of these in turn, the first choice, while easy and painless, opens your group up to problems down the road. By parting with some of your fuel, food, water, and ammo, you have reduced your own survivability. For one thing, now you're going to have to enter a zombie-infested population center to forage for the supplies you've just parted with and for another, the marauders are just going to see you as an easy mark and they'll be back with their hands out any time they need something.

The second choice isn't much better than the first. You're going to have to expend precious ammo on these losers and there's likely to be casualties in your own group. Plus, depending on how well armed they are, you could conceivably lose the fight and then where are you? If you haven't figured out that the answer is "dead", refer to Appendix E.

Believe it or not, your best option is number 3. Make sure, however, that you operate under the "keep your friends close, but your enemies closer" theory. Despite the fact that most of these people will probably turn out to be crosshair candidates, they have managed to survive up

Successful mergers of survival groups is actually a positive thing in the long run.

until now, so some of them may have skills or abilities that may be useful. If nothing else, you can use them to distract the zombies while the rest of you get away.

WHO'S HELPFUL AND WHO ISN'T:

Companionship is a basic human desire and being part of a group can have certain advantages. Different members of any group can assume specific roles based on their individual skill sets. Going it alone, on the other hand, means that you will have to be a jack-of-all-trades and able to deal with every contingency on a moment-to-moment basis. If you decide to look out only for number one, you'll eventually find yourself deep in number two. Another point to consider is what happens after the zoms have all re-died and you're left with the daunting task of having to re-build society. If all that's left is you and your shovel, we suppose you'll at least be able to dig your own grave. You won't be able to cover yourself up once you lay down, but…

Your first instinct will be to preserve those in your life significant to you and we are not here to tell anyone they should not look out for their own families and friends. This being said, anyone you intend to include in your group from the outset must be included in the planning process. It is paramount that all members of your party understand the severity of the crisis at hand and are indoctrinated in the understanding of who will be in charge when the apocalypse begins.

When choosing your companions, it must be understood that every member of the party should be able to pull their own weight and contribute to overall survivability. There should be no supercargo in your group. There is no room for sentiment when dealing with potential group members: if Uncle Charlie refuses to leave his front porch, there's no time for debate. Do not try to convince him. Accept that he has made himself a crosshair candidate and leave him behind. By the same token, despite your possible inclination to reject certain people out-of-hand (your ex, your mother-in-law, etc.); you should make an honest assessment of these people's ability to contribute to survival. Your mother-in-law may be a bitch, but if she's also a doctor, you may want to bring her along.

Let Uncle Charlie make up his own mind.

Having infants or small children in your group will entail some

particular problems (diapers come immediately to mind). Special provisions will need to be made to care for the little ones properly. This may include having members of your group whose duties are devoted entirely to childcare. To this end, we suggest... save the babysitter.

When choosing group members, it's okay to stick initially to family and friends; after all, you already know these people and have established relationships that make coexistence tolerable

You'll want a special sort of babysitter.

at the very least. However, all you can do is present the idea that you are planning for the apocalypse contingency to these people. If they laugh at you, plan around them. But realize that when the shit hits the fan, they will change their tune in a heartbeat and come knocking at your door. So assess their possible contributions anyway.

You would think that professional skill sets make for great qualifications (doctors, dentists, electricians, auto mechanics, etc.) and you would be correct in the long-run. But, if these professional people are good at their jobs, but lack the common sense to make it through the first

critical months without becoming zombie chow, what good are their professional qualifications going to be to you? What you are looking for are levelheaded individuals who can and will rise to the needs of the circumstances, can handle themselves in emergencies, won't shoot themselves in the foot when you hand them a loaded gun, and generally can be responsible for their own survival while being devoted to the group. The last thing you want in your group is a bunch of whining huddlers who expect you to take care of them and ultimately make everything okay (snivelers need not apply).

Professional ≠ survivor.

Whomever you choose to include in your group, make sure that you set up a means of communication and coordination during the first month of hiding out (remember we mentioned Ham and CB radios).

Stay in touch with pre-arranged group members as much as you can.

Once you're on the move toward your chosen long-term base, you are likely to attract the attention of additional survivors. You will have to assess these strangers on the fly, so be prepared to make some difficult decisions.

You cannot stop for everybody, in fact you may not be able to stop for anybody.

Survivors will fall into two categories: contributors and crosshair candidates. You've no doubt noticed that we have mentioned crosshair candidates several times throughout the text and perhaps you have been wondering what exactly is a crosshair candidate? Well, in a nutshell, a crosshair candidate is anyone, who through action or attitude, proves that they are more likely to be a liability than an asset to the group.

At the risk of eliciting uncomfortable groans, a crosshair candidate is anyone who might be better served in the long-run if you just shoot them now, saving them the ultimate fate of becoming zombie chow and putting them out of your misery. Hey, get a grip; this is the zombie apocalypse, not the state fair. We told you difficult choices would have to be made.

Crosshair candidates will not be hard to find (you probably know of several already). In fact, you'll most likely encounter more of them than people who'll be of use to you. Even though it seems counterintuitive, you may want to keep one or two around as zombie fodder (like "Star Trek" redshirts). Crosshair candidates will reveal themselves as such almost immediately. Signs to look for are a lack of weapons, shovel, or survival gear, an obvious pre-apocalypse mindset (i.e., walking around as if there aren't zoms everywhere), shouting or making a lot of noise, or approaching your group, making demands.

Crosshair Candidates will be abundant.

What follows is a list of personality types and attitudes that typify crosshair candidates, laid out in an easy-to-read format for your convenience. To avoid any appearance of favoritism, we are listing these examples in no particular order.

Complete Idiots

This may be the single most common type of crosshair candidate (so common in fact, that we've devoted an entire appendix to them, see Appendix E). These individuals are perfectly normal and even likable people – under ordinary circumstances. They are the people you know

from work or school, who are friendly and competent at their jobs, but are clueless outside their comfort zone. In the event of a crisis, they're among the first to panic, and without specific instructions, will have no idea what to do. For these amiable dunces, life is one long series of crosshair moments. While this is no big deal in day-to-day life, during the zombie apocalypse, these moments add up to a major train wreck. Sad as it is to say, feeding them a two-hundred-forty-grain aspirin is probably the greatest kindness you can show them.

Typical Quote: "What'll we do now?"

Aging Sixties Flower Children

This type of individual will have the hardest time adapting to a post-apocalyptic world (they spend most of their time in their own worlds anyway). They are non-violent in the extreme, even to the point of thinking that the zoms can be gotten along with (live and let un-live).

They are very group oriented and mild-mannered, but they're likely to refuse to carry a weapon under any circumstances (and when it comes to actually shooting the zoms, forget it). Thus, they will be completely dependent upon the group for their survival and are, therefore, a distinct liability. *Typical quote:* "If we show the zombies that we mean them no harm, they won't harm us."

Perky Cheerleaders

The fact that she's still wearing her uniform is your first clue that this is not someone you want in your group. A typical response by this individual to the zombies will be terrified screams and the tendency

to cling to the strongest male she can latch onto. It is highly unlikely that this person will have any survival skills and probably won't even know which end of the gun to point at the zombies. She will actually believe that she is the prettiest girl in the group, and therefore, entitled not only to protection, but to be catered to as well. There's a good chance that she'll be carrying a gym bag, but don't be fooled. It's probably just her makeup case. If she is a blonde, as well as a cheerleader, do not hesitate. Shoot! ***Typical quote:*** "eew, zombies are like, so gross. They should get makeovers."

Emos and Goths

You'll be able to recognize these individuals by their black clothes, chain-laden trip pants, and lank hair hanging in their faces. This type

is so self-absorbed that they'll hardly be aware that the zombies are even around. They will do nothing to aid the group and will barely even acknowledge anyone else's existence. Because of their overly emotional and self-destructive nature, they will typically behave in their own selfish interests (i.e., playing loud music when quiet is called for). They might even try to capture a zombie, thinking it would make a good pet. Their usefulness to the group, even as zombie fodder, is more than mitigated by their liabilities. ***Typical quote:*** "I hate the world. My life sucks. The zombies are better off than I am."

Comic-book/Sci-Fi Fanboys

These unique individuals will most likely think that the zombie apocalypse is the coolest thing that's ever happened (just like "Resident Evil"). They will see it as an opportunity to not only live the life of a zombie hunter, but to also have all the toys, comics, and DVDs they've ever wanted. Generally, their physical condition is poor and their survival skills minimal. They will have great enthusiasm for fighting zombies but no actual ability to do so. More than likely their weapon and equipment choices will be based on how cool they look instead of any practical value (check out my cool "Highlander" sword). They probably won't even have a shovel. They'll think that they're experts because they've seen every zombie movie and fantasy TV show ever

made (just like "Supernatural" episode #43). *Typical quote:* "I've seen this episode before."

Career Politicians

It's unlikely that you'll encounter any of these individuals, since chances are they'll be the victims of their own zombified security detachments. Their inability to approach even the simplest of tasks without committee meetings and hearings will stall any attempts at survival.

Regardless of their political bent, they will be convinced that they know how best to handle any situation. Any dissenting opinions will be dismissed as being obstructionist. The politician will insist on a position of leadership despite a complete unwillingness actually to take any action that accomplishes anything.
Typical quote: "We'll form a blue ribbon commission to look into this matter."

Muscle-headed Jocks

The physical prowess of these guys may seem to be an asset, but don't be fooled. They may be hot stuff on the playing field, but they're pretty useless without their playbooks. They tend to be brash, impulsive, and aggressive. They'll require a great deal of supervision, because they possess very little in the way of creative or independent thought. Without specific instructions, they'll tend to stand around doing nothing

until they're given a particular task. The only possible use for one of these guys is to send him out to break through the crowd of zombies blocking your way. He'll most likely do it without hesitation, taking the hit for the team. *Typical quote:* "You got it, Coach!"

Self-styled Zombie Hunters

Like the fanboys, this type of person will think that the zombie apocalypse is the coolest thing that's ever happened. After all, it's only now that they can shoot "people" (that is to say zoms) without fear of consequence. Generally, they will be well equipped, but will probably go through their ammunition at an alarming rate. They will be focused

more on re-killing zoms than survival. Their pursuit of their next "trophy" will tend to put them in harm's way far too often. They'll also tend to be loners and not very group oriented. Chances are good that you won't need to waste any ammo shooting these guys. By their own stupidity, they'll arrange their own demise soon enough, thereby improving the breed by natural selection. This category also includes rednecks, who think zombie re-killing is fun and military types who believe they must engage the enemy at all costs.

Typical quote: "Can you spare any ammo? I spotted a horde of zombies just a few clicks from here." Or "Can y'all spare a jug?"

Hoes, Sluts, Bimbos, Pimps and Players

These types of individuals have nothing to offer the group but empty conversation and sex (or the sale thereof). They will possess no weapons or survival gear, and their only skills will be carnal. They will regard themselves either as God's gift to the opposite sex, and therefore, worthy of your attention or as business people ready to make a simple transaction trading sexual acts for protection, resources, or commodities (If you're saying to yourself "what's wrong with that?" see Appendix E.). At first blush, this may seem like a good deal, however, these individuals will be a complete drain on your resources and will typically display a bad,

even resentful attitude toward any contribution that is not horizontal. No matter the thrills, the ride will ultimately not be worth the price of admission (and you could catch a disease). ***Typical quote:*** "You look like a nice fella, need a date?" Or "Hey there sweet-cheeks, I can rock your world."

The Arrogant Know-it-all

We all know these people and they just may be the worst type of crosshair candidate. They will never fail to give you their opinion, whether you want it or not and they will be highly offended if you disagree. They will strongly believe that they are the smartest person in any room and that they should be in charge. There's no point in attempting to argue with these individuals, no matter how civilly, because their self-righteousness is impenetrable. If you allow such a person into your group, they will spend all of their time complaining that everyone around them is doing everything wrong. In fact, they may possess skills or knowledge that might be of use to the group, but they will not be willing to put aside their own egos and think in terms of benefiting the party. In very short order, you will find them announcing their intention to leave, taking the most critical

supplies with them. They'll invite everyone to follow them, provided their leadership is accepted without question. *Typical quote:* "If you had a brain in your head, you'd admit that I'm right."

Status Conscious Egotists

These people have some personality traits in common with the arrogant know-it-alls. They're used to having everything their way and fail to understand why they're not being recognized. Conversely, they will

probably be willing to work, but will expect that special attention be paid to their contributions. They will be focused on symbols of status and so their choices will not necessarily be the most practical. Whatever their vehicle, it will have to be red and have more bells and whistles than yours. Domestic beer will not be good enough and they'll expect wine with their meals (what kind of wine goes with a shovel blade grilled cheese?). They'll be willing to wear jeans, as long as the proper brand name is splashed across their ass, but no boots will suit them unless they're completely impractical and come from an Italian designer. The monogrammed, pearl handled, nickel-plated pistol at their hip will be a clear giveaway. It won't be any good for re-killing zoms, but damn if it doesn't look good. *Typical quote:* "I am soooo thirsty, don't you have any Perrier?"

<u>Celebrities and People Too Used to Privilege</u>

People in this category share some common traits with the cheerleader and will be absolutely useless when it comes to survival. In fact, they may not have even noticed that the zombie apocalypse has been happening around them until their hunger grows intolerable because their calls for room service are yielding only an apparent busy signal. It

is only then that they will venture out in search of sustenance. Your chances of encountering any of these people are actually very slim, because they're not likely to realize that the crowds rushing toward them are zombies rather than paparazzi until it's too late. If you should encounter one of these individuals, they will not only be completely helpless and dependent upon your group, they'll also expect to be waited on hand and foot. Don't expect to get any work out of these slackers, their idea of a hard day's work is berating their servants and texting until their manicure is ruined. ***Typical quote:*** "This is why I stay out of flyover country."

The Total Slacker

This is the type of individual that has no drive or ambition. They live at home with their parents, they don't work, go to school, or do anything productive with their lives. They slouch thru life sponging off of their families and friends. Their days are spent on the couch, watching TV, or playing video games. Strangely enough, their inertia and lack of interest is precisely what will enable them to survive the initial outbreak of the ZTA, since they'll do nothing that will attract the attention of the zoms. It's most likely that several days will pass before they even realize that the zombie apocalypse is going on around them, because despite the inordinate amount of time they spend watching TV, They tend to surf past any program that seems in the least educational or informative. It's only when

they venture out to the local Quickie Mart to replenish their supply of microwave burritos and energy water that they'll get their first clue that the world has been zombified. Some of these individuals can and will rise to the occasion when it comes to survival or combatting the zoms, but their energy and interest will last only as long as the immediate crisis. They'll be useless when it comes to the day-to-day chores at the stronghold. They are the very definition of supercargo and should be avoided. ***Typical quote:*** "Eh, I'll get around to it."

As you can plainly see, crosshair candidates won't be at all hard to find. However, it must be stated that we all have moments that inspire others to roll their eyes and mutter "crosshairs". These occasional crosshair moments do not necessarily make one a crosshair candidate. It is only when these moments are a way of life that an individual merits the crosshair treatment. It's all in the attitude. If one realizes their blunder and corrects their behavior, the crosshair moments can be forgiven and the person admitted into your group.

However, in the case of true crosshair candidates, we advise that you don't waste your time on these losers. Just feed them that two-hundred-forty-grain aspirin and save yourself the headache before it starts.

CHAPTER 7: WEAPONS

Ah, now we're gettin' to the good stuff. What guns, swords, sporting goods, or farm implements are the most effective? In this chapter, we'll cover a variety of weaponry, including guns and other ranged weapons, swords and knives, clubs and blunt instruments, improvised weapons, fire, and explosives.

GUNS AND RANGED WEAPONS

When choosing a firearm, there are several factors to consider, not the least of which is how comfortable are you with your weapon. It's not a bad idea to spend some time at your local pistol/rifle range trying out a variety of guns to find out which suit you best.

When the breakdown of civilization occurs, there's an understandable temptation to arm oneself with a submachine gun and spray lead Rambo-style. This temptation must be resisted. A high rate of fire is not *necessarily* an asset.

We suggest you practice while you can.

What you want in your firearm is accuracy and knockdown power.
There is a wide variety of firearms available and all have their strengths
and weaknesses. We are not going to recommend any specific brand of
weapon (unless, of course, some enterprising gun manufacturer wants
to offer us a hefty endorsement contract...), but rather, we're going to
cover various sizes and calibers. We'll provide a brief list of pros and
cons for the various weapons discussed. The final choice is up to you
(make sure you choose wisely).

The most obvious
choice is a 9 mm
handgun. The
major advantages
of nines are that
they're easy to obtain, ammo is readily
available, and they're light and easy to
handle. On the down side, the round
is relatively light and tends to have a high muzzle
velocity and spin rate, resulting in through-and-
through wounds that do relatively little damage. This
will work against you when fighting zoms. Remember
– they don't feel pain. .38s have several characteristics
in common with nines, including a lack of knockdown power.
Consequently, if you are not a particularly good shot with a handgun,
these two may not be your best choices.

Exotic guns like Desert Eagles, Mausers, or Webleys are not
recommended. They tend to be high maintenance (the Desert Eagle),

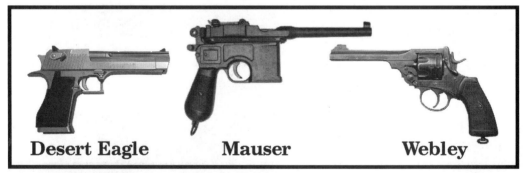

Desert Eagle   **Mauser**   **Webley**

replacement parts are scarce (the Mauser), or the ammo is virtually
nonexistent (the Webley ".454 caliber? Are you kidding!"). However, if
you want to carry one of these just because they look so damn cool, we
refer you to Appendix E.

Unless you're an expert on gun repair (or even if you are), our best advice on choosing firearms is: keep it simple. For handguns, your best choices are heavy revolvers: .357s, .44s or .45s are best. The ammunition is common; they're durable, accurate, and low maintenance. Plus,

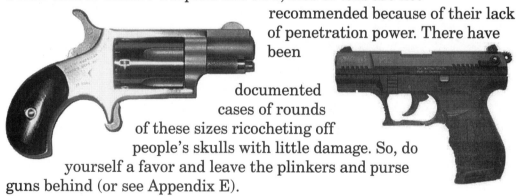

even if you miss your initial headshot and hit the zombie in the shoulder, that two-hundred-forty-grain round is going to blow its arm off (which should at least slow it down). The downside, of course, is their limited capacity. So, you'll probably want to carry more than one (highly advisable). One tip though: Make sure your handguns are all the same caliber. That way, you only need to carry one type of ammunition.

Small caliber rimfire weapons like .22s, .25s or .32s are not recommended because of their lack of penetration power. There have been

documented cases of rounds of these sizes ricocheting off people's skulls with little damage. So, do yourself a favor and leave the plinkers and purse guns behind (or see Appendix E).

When choosing a long gun, our advice is not to over think it. Bolt-action hunting or sniper rifles are great over long distances, but less effective

German made, bolt action, modern hunting rifle.

in closer quarters. Automatic weapons (submachine guns and assault rifles) require training and practice to handle properly. You need to

make an honest
assessment of
whether or not
you can actually
use them competently (if
not, don't). Semi-automatic or lever action
rifles are probably your best options in
terms of versatility and overall handling. Just

make sure that your
choice uses a heavy round (NO RABBIT GUNS!).

Until you reach and fortify your stronghold, fixed emplacement
weapons, such as heavy machine guns, mortars, and the like should be
used sparingly. They take too long to set up and are too heavy to schlep
around with you easily. When on the move, the only practical use for
machine guns is to mount them on your vehicle(s).

Shotguns are devastating at close range but lose power over distance.
They should be considered weapons of last resort. In fact, you may want
to save one of those rounds for yourself. On the other hand, a shotgun
with a rifled slug barrel may be just the thing. The rifling will increase

the weapon's range to as much as two hundred yards and a headshot with one of those twelve-gauge slugs will effectively decapitate the zom. Yes, we know that rifled shotguns are more expensive, but as previously stated, this is no time to pinch pennies.

TENSIONED STRING WEAPONS

Bows and crossbows are highly effective in the hands of an expert. They have the advantages of being virtually silent and extremely low maintenance. However, their single-shot capacity makes them of little use against a zombie horde. Slingshots, in addition to having

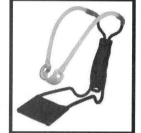

the same limitations as bows and crossbows, lack penetration power and are not recommended.

SWORDS AND KNIVES

Bladed weapons can be very useful for melee combat. However, it must be stressed that hand-to-hand combat with zombies is not advisable. Unfortunately, it sometimes cannot be avoided, so it's best to be prepared.

When selecting your blade, you want one light enough to swing easily, but heavy enough to decapitate a zom with one blow. Your best option is a katana, saber, or other long sword with a high quality, carbon-steel

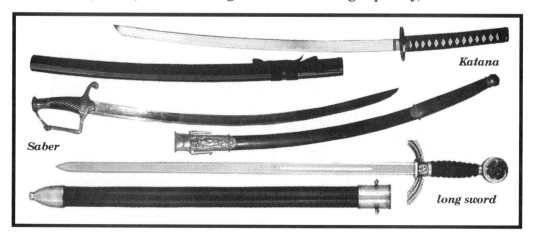

Katana

Saber

long sword

blade. Keep in mind, however, that enclosed environments severely curtail their effectiveness. Therefore, a short sword, such as a Roman gladius or a wakizashi, is an excellent back up. A large Bowie/survival

Roman Gladius

Wakizashi

Bowie

Tanto

knife or tanto can be useful in a pinch. Overly large swords like claymores should be avoided because: a) their large size and weight make them difficult to carry, and b) they require a great deal of strength and endurance to wield for any length of time.

Machetes can be highly effective. Just make sure you get one made from quality steel. Avoid cheap pot metal machetes from the gardening store as they lack tensile strength and cutting power. The last thing you want is for your blade to break or get stuck halfway through the zombie's neck. Axes, despite their heavy skull crushing power, have an unfortunate tendency to get stuck in said skulls at crucial moments, and consequently, should be avoided.

CLUBS AND BLUNT INSTRUMENTS

Zombies are highly susceptible to head trauma, so a club can be useful. However, it takes a very strong individual to wield one with sufficient force to re-kill a zom. If you are such a person, make sure you choose the best club. Baseball bats are an okay choice but not the best. Wooden bats are preferable to aluminum because: a) they're heavier, and b) that solid piece of ash makes a very satisfying crack when impacting with a zom's skull. Your best options when choosing a club are either a medieval mace or if you own a wood lathe, get a large, solid piece of hardwood-oak or walnut- and make the club yourself (if it was good enough for Buford Pusser...).

IMPROVISED WEAPONS

If you have properly prepared, this should not be an issue, but sometimes the unexpected happens, so you need to think on your feet. The following are just a few examples.

Bad choices:

Golf club - the narrow shaft will bend or break
Rolling pin - too short, not heavy enough
Chainsaw - needs gas, fails to start at a crucial moment
Hedge trimmer - NEEDS ELECTRICITY! (Or see chainsaws!)
Hedge shears - do we really need to explain this one?
Scythes and sickles - blades dull too quickly
Lawn mowers - see chainsaws (besides, have you ever tried to lift a lawn mower!)

Good choices:

Tire irons, crowbars or *steel pipes* (no PVC!) - are excellent skull crushers
Banjos or *electric guitars* - work great until the neck breaks
Steam iron - just swing it around on its cord
Cast iron cookware - large skillets are best
Meat cleavers - be careful though, they tend to get stuck
Sledgehammer - If you've got the stamina, go for it!

FIRE AND EXPLOSIVES

If you can get your hands on explosives before the apocalypse, great; however, most people will have to wait until civilization collapses. TNT or dynamite is an excellent choice for an explosive (C-4 or Semtex are

also good but harder to find). It's highly stable, travels well, and will be relatively easy to obtain (construction companies and mining concerns generally have a good supply). If you can make your way onto an abandoned military base, you will find many useful items of ordinance. You will want to concentrate primarily on anti-personnel devices, such as hand grenades (fragmentation, incendiary, or high explosive) or mines (claymores, etc.). Keep in mind that mines, like machine guns, are only useful for defending fixed locations and should be used sparingly while you're on the move.

Only use fire when you can trap the zombies. If they're still able to attack, fire will work against you. Think about it; zombies are bad enough. Do you really want to deal with one that's on fire? However, when it's appropriate, some of your best choices for incendiary devices are: Thermite grenades, napalm, and Molotov cocktails. The major advantage of Molotov cocktails is the ease with which they can be procured. Alcohol will be available by the case (eighty proof or better is recommended), then all you need to do is add a wick – any piece of alcohol soaked cloth will do – flick your Bic and let fly.

Rocket or grenade launchers are highly effective, but should only be used against crowds of zoms (no sense in wasting a perfectly good explosion on only one or two) and from a safe distance. You'll want to stick with anti-personnel rounds (fragmentation, flechette, high explosive, or incendiary). Armor piercing rounds would just be overkill (or is that over re-kill?).

OTHER WEAPONS

We know that there are those out there who are wondering about things like spears, shurikens, boomerangs, and the like. To them we say; this is the zombie apocalypse not a ninja movie. If you want to carry that crap, see Appendix E.

Note:

It is important to remember that like all your equipment, your weapons require care and maintenance. So, make sure you keep the proper cleaning kits, oils, and sharpening tools in your supplies. If you take care of your weapons, they'll take care of you.

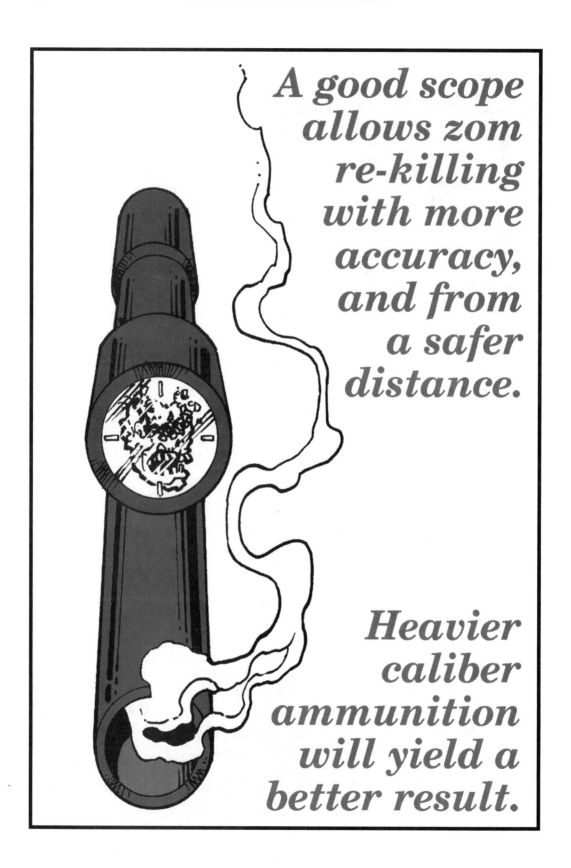

A good scope allows zom re-killing with more accuracy, and from a safer distance.

Heavier caliber ammunition will yield a better result.

CHAPTER 8: COMBAT

The objective of this manual is to survive the zombie apocalypse, so your best bet is to avoid zombies whenever possible. However, since zombies will outnumber you literally millions to one, some encounters are inevitable, so you need to know what to do.

The most obvious way to re-kill a zom is to shoot it in the head. Ideally, this should be done from a secure location, using a rifle with a scope. That said, in the zombie apocalypse things will rarely be ideal, so on to plan "B".

Your rifle should still be your primary weapon. You'll want to keep as much distance between yourself and the zoms as possible. The first rule is *don't panic*. Firing rounds wildly or blindly is counterproductive and wastes ammunition. Calm methodical headshots are what are called for. Take your time and do it right.

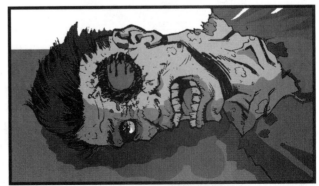

Any clear headshot will re-kill a zom.

When using handguns, it must be remembered that the most *effective* range for most handguns is fifteen to twenty-five feet. So, don't start firing until the zoms are within that range. As with using your rifle, calm methodology is what's called for. Taking that extra half-second to aim properly will most likely save your life.

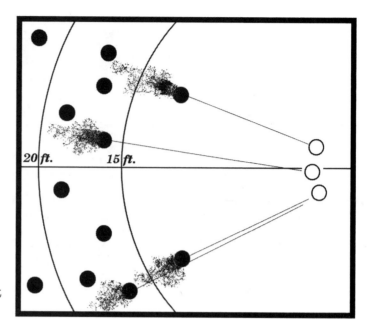

If you are using automatic weapons, it is vital that you maintain fire discipline. The last thing you want is for your magazine to run dry when you need it the most. Fire only in short bursts and only when the zoms are within effective range (similar to that of handguns).

It's possible that the zoms might get too close to use your guns effectively or you'll run out of ammo, despite your best intentions. That's when you'll need to rely on your sword(s). The best target for

A good grip is essential.

your blade is the zom's neck. Use smooth strong swings, not panicked hacking. Clean decapitations are what you're going for here. Good alternative targets are the zom's legs. That's right, we said the legs (why the legs, we hear you cry). The object of the exercise is to survive the apocalypse, not re-kill zoms. So, by removing a zom's legs you will slow it down considerably (and the others will trip over it), giving you a chance to escape. Running away from zombies isn't cowardice, it's just good sense.

Your brain is your biggest asset in a fight with zombies. As previously stated, you are alive, the zombies aren't. Therefore, it's a relatively simple matter to trap them so you can re-kill them with minimal personal risk. For example, you set up a series of napalm canisters (available at most air force bases) in a quarry with remote detonators. Then, add a battery powered sound system with a strobe light (zombies are attracted to light, sound, and movement), crank up the volume, turn it on, and clear the area (use binoculars to observe from a safe location).

Then, when the quarry is filled shoulder-to-shoulder with zombies, you set off your charges in sequence and poof – zombie flambé! The beauty of this plan is that you don't even need to hide your explosives. The zombies won't notice them.

A good explosion can be very satisfying.

COMBAT TIPS:

1) Know your battlefield. Familiarize yourself with the terrain as much as possible, so you can use it to your best advantage.
2) Keep moving. Most zombies are slow and ponderous. Make good use of your superior speed and agility.
3) Prioritize your targets. Newly turned zombies are faster and more functional than older ones. So, shoot the fast ones first.
4) Don't be sentimental. It doesn't matter if the zombie was your parent, sibling, child, spouse, or best friend. It's a zombie now and the only good zombie is a re-dead zombie. Shoot!
5) Don't fight alone. Having at least one partner with you will enable you to watch each other's backs.
6) Leave yourself a way out. Never allow yourself to be surrounded or backed into a corner.

This last one raises the inevitable question: What do you do if you find yourself weaponless and surrounded by zoms, with no hope of escape? Look at the bright side. At least life has been good to you up until now. If, on the other hand, life hasn't been good to you (which, given your present situation, seems more likely), look at the bright side. At least you won't be bothered by it for much longer.

A war of attrition against zombies is not only unwinnable, but unnecessary. Zombies will decompose in a matter of months, ending their threat. Your goal is to reach and fortify your stronghold. Then you just need to wait it out. Anyone who aspires to be a zombie hunter is a crosshair candidate and is referred to Appendix E. So, stay cautious, stay alert, and stay alive.

Zombie hunter = Crosshair candidate.

CHAPTER 9: THE DO'S AND DON'TS OF SURVIVAL

The zombie apocalypse is indeed survivable. This entire manual, thus far, has been devoted to giving you the exact information you need to ensure your own survival and that of your family and friends. Still, there may be things so simple, they are easily overlooked; things that might qualify you as a crosshair candidate if you happened to forget enough of them. Your goal should be to make remembering these things second nature, so that when the zoms rise, you'll instantly know what and what not to do.

The ability to think on your feet is vital to survival, and you don't want to be caught dithering when the zoms attack. This is especially true when dealing with first-stage zoms. They're fast and extremely deadly, and won't give you a moment to catch your breath. You'll want your reactions to be instinctive and decisive.

If you do the wrong thing, it can sometimes turn out worse than if you do nothing. It's the bad decisions that lead to the dreaded catastrophic crosshair moment. In order to minimize this risk, we've included the following handy quick reference list of "do's and don'ts". We would strongly suggest that you study them carefully and commit them to memory because when the zombie apocalypse hits, the zoms will not give an opportunity to the look these things up on the run.

DO

Make a thourough study of the text and follow it's instructions.

DON'T

Try to look up what to do while the zombies are chasing you.

DO

Start planning for the apocalypse now.

DON'T

Wait until the zombies rise.

DO
Zombie-proof your home as soon as possible.

DON'T
Attempt to board up the windows as the zombies are climbing through them.

DO
Stock what you really need.

DON'T
Plan like it's a party.

DO Pick a large sturdy vehicle.

DON'T Go for the hybrid.

DO Travel with people who can actually help you.

DON'T Pick up crosshair candidates.

DO Choose what really works. Pack some serious firepower.

DON'T Arm yourself like you're in a ninja movie.

DO Shoot the fast zombies first.

DON'T Pick off the easy targets.

DO Fire from a distance.

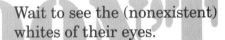
DON'T Wait to see the (nonexistent) whites of their eyes.

DO Approach and negotiate safely and cautiously.

DON'T welcome all comers with open arms.

Take back up with you to the bathroom.

Go it alone.

Keep your shovel handy.

Get caught empty handed.

DO

Run away from the swarming zombies as fast as you can.

DON'T

Try to help someone who's being attacked by zombies. It's too late for them anyway.

DO

Encourage all your friends and family to buy this book.

DON'T

Lend out your copy.

CHAPTER 10: A THEORETICAL TIME LINE

In the ongoing text we've covered a wide variety of subjects, ranging from just what is a zombie, to planning and preparation, supplies, where to go and how to get there, who to travel with, what weapons to use, how to fight zombies, how to handle other survivors, and even some specific do's and don'ts. Now it is time to lay this whole apocalypse out for you in an easy to understand time line.

From our discussion of un-life expectancy, you will recall that the average zombie can exist for as long as a year. In the vast majority of cases and in most geographical locations, a year is actually rather unlikely, but that makes it a safe time period to consider from a survival perspective.

So holding out one year is the goal for survival to be safely completed. Let's now look at a survival scenario from the standpoint of what you should do and consider as you navigate your way through the zombie apocalypse.

To begin, we will assume that you will, in fact, act upon the planning and preparation suggestions so that when the zombies rise, you will at the very least have made some plans regarding where resources may be located and how you will eventually get to them.

DAY ZERO: OUTBREAK

As has been suggested, the catalyst of the zombie apocalypse could take a few different forms. If for instance, some unknown, widespread phenomenon causes the initial outbreak (rogue comet or mysterious green mist theories) then the effect will be a huge number of zombies created all at once. Some sort of biological warfare might have a similar effect. However, we feel that the more likely scenario is that the ZTA will be some sort of naturally occurring mutated virus, which will very likely begin with a single first victim.

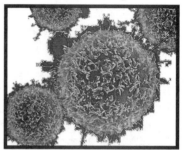

The ZTA could be a virus.

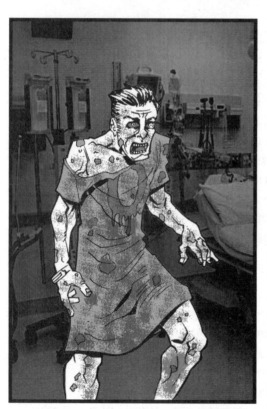

Using this as our model, we will assume that patient zero contracted the ZTA and the resultant illness drove him or her to some sort of medical center for assistance. No matter the city or country, this location is one where people will be gathered in close proximity. Regardless of the time it takes for the ZTA to cause this first victim's death, from the moment that the first zombie rises into un-life, the apocalypse will have begun. Due to the extremely aggressive nature of this first stage zombie, it can be assumed that it will succeed in transferring the ZTA to at least a half dozen victims before any coherent action is taken to contain or re-kill it. Re-killing would be preferable, but in their ignorance, these first humans to encounter the zombie cannot be counted upon to recognize what is actually happening.

As the first mortally wounded victims turn, the apocalypse will begin to grow at a phenomenal rate. By the end of day zero, we estimate that the ZTA will consume no less than 50% of the population center where the apocalypse begins. Any semblance of social order will be completely given over to anarchy, and any survivors (excepting those who have purchased and read this book – and prepared of course) will be desperately fighting for their lives in a struggle they will ultimately lose or hiding in some place they will eventually be forced to abandon for hunger's sake.

For the readers of this book – if you are unfortunate enough to live near ground zero – at the very first indication of trouble, head to your fortified home. It's best if you can be in your secure location before you encounter any zombies. If possible, listen to a local radio station and monitor the TV so that when the first stories begin to break, you'll be able to interpret the confusion properly. Armed with the knowledge of Zombology 101, you should be able to recognize the key factors being reported and take immediate action. Calmly head for your vehicle and go directly home. Use a route that avoids airports, hospitals, and high congestion centers. Contact other designated members of your party and generally prepare to wait it out.

If you don't live near ground zero, you may not get clear news of events until day one, but don't panic, you'll still have the advantage of knowledge and a plan.

DAY ONE: CONFUSION

On the first full day of the apocalypse, the government will respond. There will be an attempt to throw a civil net around the problem but the exodus from the center place will be completely panic driven and uncontainable. Plus, due to the incredible mobility of modern society, the problem will already be spreading internationally. The decision will be made to mobilize a military attempt at containment. A political struggle will ensue between the generals who want to eliminate the problem with WMDs (Weapons of Mass Destruction) and the scientists who will want to study it.

The panic and confusion will be so wide-spread that no containment will be possible.

Meanwhile, outbreaks will be popping up in cities around the globe at international airports and at medical facilities near these travel focal points. At each location of outbreak, the result will be a repeat of Day Zero.

Because of the speed of outbreak, no one will know about patient zero and the authorities will be completely in the dark about what they're dealing with. Governments, unable to act without that knowledge or a responsible enemy, will wallow in confusion. The first day will end with several major cities in various countries completely overrun with all civil attempts at control completely failing.

If you don't get your first indications of local trouble until Day One, it's okay. When you get your first credible reports of trouble, follow the directions given previously. Go home, contact all members of your group, and prepare to wait it out.

DAY TWO: REALIZATION

By the morning of the second day, the ZTA will have spread epidemically. Complete cities will have been abandoned as unrecoverable, and the effected government bodies will realize that they are dealing with something beyond a terrorist attack, as all their enemies are dealing with the same crisis. Panicked and unprepared, the governments will direct their militaries to take action both to contain the problem and to eliminate the threat. All of these efforts will be useless, as the military

There is no nuclear option against the ZTA.

infrastructure will already be internally affected. There is the possibility that a few cities will be bombed in a last-ditch effort to solve the problem. Whatever military forces succeed at carrying out such an action, inevitably will see the futility of it so it's unlikely to occur on a large scale.

Heads of government will be whisked away to their presumed secure locations, but as these are usually large-scale facilities requiring dozens of support and security personnel, the likelihood is great that the ZTA will find its way in. It is after all government and not well known for clear situational understanding or decisive action.

First responders = Appetizers

Territorial and local governments will be trying to act as well. Emergency services will be mobilized, achieving nothing but guaranteeing their total demise or zombification. Various forms of martial law will be declared, none having any positive effect whatsoever.

By Day Two, you'll be safely secured in your home, enjoying the fruits of your planning, and keeping a watchful eye on the goings on around you. It won't be easy or in any way pleasant to witness the breakdown of society and the outright killing of your neighbors and community, but remember, it's beyond the time for sentiment. Now is the time to stay secure and quiet and ensure your own survival.

DAY THREE: ACCEPTANCE

By Day Three, most of the major population centers will have succumbed to the ZTA. The media will have fallen silent except for spotty disjointed broadcasts from local stations. If there's any final advice from any sort of authority figure before the technological world falls silent, it will most likely be to stay in your homes and wait. (Actually not bad advice if it had come earlier with instructions to be prepared to wait about a month.)

The internet will be ablaze with speculation and un-provable theories and there will be pages and pages of advice on just what to do. These posts, however, will dwindle dramatically as the ZTA spreads. As each blogger disappears, it can be assumed that they have succumbed. Whole sections of electronic infrastructure will begin failing and the internet will cease to be, as servers are interrupted or damaged on a worldwide scale. While the basic electrical grid may continue for some time before catastrophic failure, there will certainly be areas of blackout. Likewise, the municipal water systems may continue for several months before catastrophic failure; however, the water may no longer be potable within as little as two days. Be sure to assess carefully any tap water before use.

As chaos reigns around you, you'll be able to laugh at this absurdity as you sit comfortably in your prepared domicile re-reading this manual. So warm up an MRE, pour yourself a glass of whatever is your preferred comfort drink, and enjoy the entertainment factor of the end of civilization for as long as it lasts.

If you happened to be at ground zero, the world will have grown oddly silent. If you have arranged a means of outside observation, you may see the occasional shuffling zom, but if you do nothing to attract its attention, it will most likely continue on its way. While zoms are able to detect living humans at close proximity, you are in little danger of detection from a distance as long as you do nothing to draw attention. Many people who have survived thus far simply by taking hasty unprepared shelter, will have reached the point where their need for food and water (and weapons) will be driving them to abandon their

initial security. Bolstered by the apparent silence, they will venture out in search of answers and assistance. These poor ignorant crosshair candidates will become a second wave of fresh zombies.

This scenario will continue to repeat itself over the next few days, as survivors, having been unprepared for the zombies' rise, venture out of hiding, lured by the silence to think that the danger may have passed.

At this point, the ZTA will still be spreading, overtaking the entire globe at an alarming rate. Governments will have failed or be failing, and most military and emergency services will have given up any attempts to respond, turning finally to thoughts of their own survival. However, for the vast majority, it will already be too late.

There will have been no time for widespread looting, so resources should be, for the most part, untouched. You'll now just need to hunker down, stay quiet, and wait until it is relatively safe to move to your chosen stronghold location.

ONE WEEK OUT: THE INTERNATIONAL HOUSE OF ZOMS

By one week, the zombie apocalypse will be a worldwide phenomenon. There will certainly be remote places in the world that have not yet been touched, but almost no place will be immune. Any such place that remains as remote to outsiders as to survive the zombie apocalypse will certainly be of no help to you, nor is it likely to pose any threat to any future rebuilding efforts.

All local, state, territorial, and national governments will have failed. Military structures will have been compromised and zombified, along with everything else. Desolation will reign as the zoms wander in search of survivors. The zoms themselves will likely be beyond their first stage, reduced now to shambling, halting heaps. There will still be first-stage zoms about as new bands of unwitting and unprepared survivors give up their locations intentionally or otherwise.

The world will be a quiet place. The electricity may not yet have failed, but all broadcasts will have ceased (accept for the CB and Ham radio operators who have read this manual and are following its instructions). You may not have seen any zoms for a couple of days, but don't believe for a moment that they're not out there.

TWO WEEKS OUT: CONSTANT VIGILANCE

You may not have seen or heard anything for several days, but stay the course. The last thing you want to do is reveal your location before you're ready. Staying in communication with the designated members of your party in different locations may serve to bolster your spirits but do  so sparingly, as any sound could potentially compromise your location.

If you have a safe observation place or better yet an electronic means of surveillance, then monitor your surroundings carefully, but do your best to keep yourself and your party occupied and quiet. Do not allow the silence or apparent inactivity to lure you into changing your schedule.

When you're ready to make your move, you want to be reasonably certain that there will be no first-stage zombies about to pursue you.

The world has succumbed now to the zombie apocalypse. Make no mistake of thinking otherwise. There may well be other survivors out there. Some prepared like yourself and others hapless, miraculously lucky crosshair candidates. But they will not be many compared to the number of wandering zoms. Your survival is far from guaranteed at this point (unless you own this book of course), so continue to be vigilant and stick to your plan.

ONE MONTH OUT: MOVING DAY
So, you have stuck to your plan and made it to moving day. For one month, you have survived in your closed up home and now you're ready to go somewhere else. The house will stink, the garbage will be piled up (hadn't thought about that had you?), you may not have had a shower in a while if the municipal water has failed, and if the electricity has failed, it will have been a long wait. In actuality, it is quite likely that the electrical grid is still functioning, even after four unattended weeks. Localized blackouts would have happened to be sure, but they can be the result of many sorts of disturbances. If you have had the means to observe outside your home, you may have been able to see if lights are still in operation in other places. In any case, the grid may have already failed and if it hasn't, it certainly could experience catastrophic failure at any time, so a little haste would be a good thing.

Once you start preparing to leave, you will make enough noise that you will almost certainly attract the attention of the zoms. This is why we suggest that you have a prepared vehicle in an attached garage, so that you can safely transfer passengers and gear.

Be certain you can access your vehicle safely. A secured attached garage is ideal.

Now, this is when your personal plan comes into play. You should have picked a location to be your stronghold, you should have cased it well, and know its points of exit and entrance. You should have planned your point of entry and either brought with you, or pre-planned, based on knowledge of the contents of your chosen stronghold, everything you'll need to secure the entrance once you have gotten your party and yourself inside.

Be sure to coordinate departure and arrival times with any other members of your party at other locations (remember the CB/Ham radios?) then it'll be time to leave. Before you start the engine, it's a good idea to turn on a loud stereo at the furthest point of your home, put in a CD with lots of bass, and put it on repeat. This will draw the zoms away from your garage door toward the sound source. Once you have given this a few minutes to work, start your engine and be sure it's running smoothly before you open the garage door. The best scenario is to have rigged an electric garage door opener to work from a battery source so that no one will have to be outside your vehicle to open the door. (If the electricity is still on, you're good, but you should have rigged it before hand to be safe.) Once the door is open, just drive through any approaching zoms and out onto the road. At this point, the likelihood of there being any first-stage zombies is extremely slim, so you should only have to deal with slow ambling corpses. These will offer very little resistance to being driven through and over.

Proceed along your pre-planned route to a designated rendezvous point outside your stronghold location. This is the most likely time that you will encounter other survivors not part of your coordinated party. People may run out of homes and other buildings and attempt to flag you down. Use your best judgment and knowledge of how much actual space you have to determine whether you wish to stop for any of these survivors or not. If they seem to not be in a panic and follow you in a vehicle of their own, they may be worth assessing at a safer time. Otherwise, choose safely and carefully and do not hesitate to administer the two-hundred-forty-grain aspirin mercifully where it makes the most sense.

Any operating vehicles will attract the attention of the zoms, so keep in constant communication with your party so that arrival at the rendezvous point is coordinated and simultaneous. This point should be at an observation distance from the entrance you wish to use to enter

your chosen stronghold and in an area relatively clear of zoms. Take a couple of minutes to quickly review assigned tasks and assess your chosen entrance location for the proximity of zoms. If there are a large number of zoms in the area, set your zombie lures (as described in chapter 3) and drive away in the opposite direction. Drive a good distance away before doubling back to come around and approach your entrance from another direction. Give the lure, or lures, plenty of time to work (at least twenty minutes).

Once you arrive at the designated entrance, pull your vehicles end-to-end to create a barrier and offload from one side only. Move directly to your entrance. Do what is necessary to gain entry. If the facility has been locked, this is a very good thing because it minimizes the likelihood of numerous zombies being inside. If an electronic door has

been in operation, then be prepared to deal with a shit-load of zoms. Nevertheless, send in members of your party best equipped to clear the facility, quickly offload any necessary gear, and secure the entrance. (For further guidance, refer back to chapter 3.) If the area is relatively zombie free when you arrive, you should have time to quickly accomplish these tasks, just make sure that members of your party are posted as lookouts so that any zoms can be picked off before becoming a threat.

Once your party has gained and secured entrance, wait together for the all clear from the anti-zom patrol. When given, you can begin the tasks of securing, coordinating, and modifying your stronghold for long-term occupation. (See chapter 3 for information on this activity.)

Life within your stronghold should be far more pleasant than the first month holed up silently in your home. Here, you'll have the camaraderie of your chosen companions, as well as greater resources, and the facility should be secured enough from the zoms that you can move about freely and make noise as you wish without fear of infiltration.

Congratulations... your survival looks fairly well secured at this point.

TWO MONTHS OUT: OPERATING FROM YOUR BASE

After a full two months, the zombies will have wandered into every corner of the Earth, spreading the ZTA. The only places that may have escaped are remote villages in the deepest jungles or in the highest mountains surrounded by rugged terrain. Places that already have very little contact with the outside world. The people there will not be worried about what is happening to the rest of humanity. Their lives will go on unchanged and perhaps even slightly for the better.

The rest of the world will have become quiet and still. By two months, the power grids will have experienced catastrophic failure and have gone down completely. Water systems will also have failed. While the sewerage system will still be viable for what little use your party will place on it; there will no longer be water pressure and nothing flowing from the tap. (At your stronghold, this can be fixed by sinking a well and installing pumps. See chapter 2.)

Your presence will have attracted considerable attention from the zombies around you and you may have developed quite a crowd outside the walls of your stronghold. You could deal with this by dumping barrels of flammable liquid down into the gathered horde and igniting them from above. As the zoms at this point will be incredibly slow, this is an effective means of re-killing any that are gathered in large numbers.

By now (depending on the size of your group) you'll probably be experiencing some shortages of certain supplies, fuel, foodstuffs, and so on. Now is the time to begin sending out foraging teams to establish re-supply locations and assess zombie population. These teams, with a little planning, can also begin to do some routine zombie trapping and elimination (see chapter 8.) It won't hurt to spend a little time clearing traffic lanes along the main routes from your stronghold to wherever you're getting and possibly storing resources, such as fuel. The heavy construction equipment needed to do this, while not recommended as safe transportation earlier on, may now be just what you need for certain applications. Just remember that you should always buddy up, so that one person can watch for zoms as the other performs whatever task is at hand.

Long-range planning will now be at the top of your list, as life with the zoms will have fallen into a bit of a routine. Hopefully, with enough entrapment and elimination sessions, you'll have considerably cut down on the number of zoms wandering around you. At this point, it is not advisable to wander any farther than is necessary from your stronghold.

You should have planned ahead and know just where each type of resource is located. Wandering far afield into what was once a highly populated area should still be considered unsafe. Let the zoms come to you and practice careful methods of re-killing them when they do. Never go out 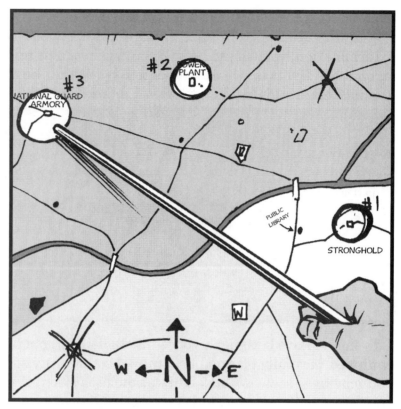 looking for populations of zoms. To do so would be to put your entire party at unnecessary risk and make you a prime crosshair candidate, giving some other member of your party the clear invitation to feed you a two-hundred-forty-grain aspirin.

You still need to be very careful whenever you venture outside your stronghold walls, but some activities will be required to maintain the support of the group.

If you have been lucky, your contact with thieves and marauders will have been very little and you will have followed the instructions of chapter 6 in dealing with these additional threats.

If you live in a northern climate, you may be engaged in serious winter planning, as the cold will create additional survival obstacles. The only upside to this sort of climate zone is that a full-out winter should re-kill the zombies on a large scale. Just be sure to deal with these re-dead bodies properly come the thaw, as they may still retain the ability to pass on the ZTA under certain circumstances.

SIX MONTHS OUT: PLANNING FOR THE FUTURE

If you have been well organized and practiced a good program of zombie extermination, you should be seeing very few zoms approaching your stronghold. But it is still advisable to have round the clock surveillance and pick off any approaching zoms at a fair distance.

Life should have become fairly comfortable and hopeful for your well-equipped, carefully planned program of community survival. In fact, you may have seen established relationships strengthened and, if your stronghold population is large enough (assuming other survivors have joined your ranks); you may also have seen new relationships established. You may even see your population grow through natural human reproduction. These are good signs for future prosperity.

It is a good idea at some point to have established a stop at a large public library and added this resource to your own. With an organized effort at learning, you can assign individuals or small groups with uncovering knowledge that you will eventually need for enhanced survival. If you have younger survivors amongst your group, this is also an important resource for both basic learning and entertainment.

Now is the time to cement the social order within your group. If possible, carefully fit group members to tasks that they may find fulfilling. Encourage group activities and inclusive forms of entertainment, as you cannot afford to have loners amongst your company.

When the day comes that you can open the stronghold and declare it is safe to move outward and rebuild a greater society, you want this to happen with a bit of hesitancy, not for fear of zombies, but for a real and true attachment to the larger group. Promoting this dynamic will serve the larger community in the future.

If you are heading into winter, use your time wisely, gathering the supplies you will need to last through bitter weather without having to venture out. Planning for the spring will be the best use of winter down time.

If you are coming out of winter you will likely be gearing up for spring planting, including plans for obtaining the equipment necessary and perhaps even planning to clear and reclaim land to keep your planting close by.

You will be half way toward your stated goal, and this should cause morale to run high within your group. Celebrate this, honor holidays, and remember life as it was before the rise of the zoms. The second half of the year is more likely to run smoothly if you have planned well up to this point.

You must remember though, that you are not quite there yet and the unexpected could still happen, so we suggest you watch for it.

ONE YEAR: CONGRATULATIONS, YOU'VE SURVIVED

By this point, you will have not seen a zombie in quite some time and if you're very lucky, you never will again. It is quite likely that most of the zoms have expired, many having become food for scavenging animals and packs of feral dogs. But it is a good idea, as you move outward from your stronghold to begin the business of building your post-apocalyptic life, that you remain vigilant, always carry appropriate weaponry, and don't forget your shovel!

Much will need to be done (agriculture comes immediately to mind), as you will not be able to eat canned food forever. Just be sure, as you move outward to explore and search for additional resources and perhaps even other survivors in other strongholds, that you carefully dismantle whatever anti-personnel defenses you have installed. You are now an official survivor of the zombie apocalypse, it wouldn't do to become the first survivor to have a catastrophic crosshairs moment and step on one of your own landmines.

CHAPTER 11: CONCLUSIONS

Let's review what we've learned.

1) The zombie apocalypse is coming. Probably when it's least convenient.

2) Zombies are dead. It's only through the influence of the ZTA that they have any semblance of life.

3) Having a plan is vital. No plan results in zombification.

4) Being prepared is your best defense. Being part of the rioting crowd at the local Quickie Mart is just asking to be zombie chow.

5) Assemble a proper cache of supplies. This is the zombie apocalypse, not a New Year's Eve party.

6) Choosing the correct vehicle and properly zombie proofing it is a must. Anything less will make you zombie drive-thru.

7) Choose your companions wisely and avoid crosshair candidates.

8)   Be practical in your weapon choices. Aesthetics is not a factor in picking your weapons. What matters is how re-deadly they are.

9)   Avoid zoms whenever possible. But, if you must shoot, shoot to re-kill.

10)   The zombies will rise with incredible rapidity. Within a couple of weeks, the zoms will overrun the world. Within a year, they'll be gone. Now, that's a fast-paced life (well, actually, un-life).

There you have it. We've given you all the information you'll need to survive the zombie apocalypse. If you're not a crosshair candidate, you'll act on it. If you are, you'll ignore it and end up zombie chow (no big loss). We'll be waiting in our well-secured bunker and we'll see you after the last zoms are re-dead. Until then, keep your guns loaded and your shovel handy!

GOT SHOVEL?

TEST YOUR SURVIVAL KNOWLEDGE (answers and scoring on pg., 153)

What follows is a short quiz. Do you have what it takes? Are you a survivor or a crosshair candidate?

NOTE: Please use a No, 2 pencil only, and completely fill in the corresponding oval.

1) What is the best way to re-kill a zombie?

   ○ A) Set it on fire.   ○ B) Decapitate it.

   ○ C) Shoot it in the head.   ○ D) Poke it in the eye with a sharp stick.

2) What is your best zombie apocalypse vehicle?

   ○ A) A boat.   ○ B) An M-1 Abrams tank.

   ○ C) A motorcycle.   ○ D) A 4WD SUV with a snowplow.

3) What term best describes a zombie?

   ○ A) Re-dead.   ○ B) Un-live.

   ○ C) Mostly dead.   ○ D) Undead.

4) What is your best long-range weapon?

   ○ A) Bow and arrow.   ○ B) A handgun.

   ○ C) A rifle with a scope.   ○ D) A boomerang.

5) What does ZTA mean?

   ○ A) Zombie Total Annihilation.   ○ B) Zombie Transit Authority.

   ○ C) Zombie Tactical Attrition.   ○ D) Zombie Transforming Agent.

6) Which is your best improvised weapon?

   ○ A) A sledgehammer.   ○ B) A golf club

   ○ C) A lawn mower.   ○ D) A Banjo.

7) Which is the best base camp?

   ○ A) A tree house.   ○ B) A warehouse club store.

   ○ C) Your own home.   ○ D) A post office.

8) What's the best all-around tool to carry?

   ○ A) A pipe wrench.   ○ B) A crowbar.

   ○ C) A shovel.   ○ D) A corkscrew.

9) What is the best CD to use in a zombie lure?

   ○ A) Led Zeppelin's "ZoSo".   ○ B) Michael Jackson's "Thriller".

   ○ C) "Sounds of the rain forest".   ○ D) Yanni's "In celebration of life".

10) What is your best melee weapon?

   ○ A) A Katana.   ○ B) A Bowie knife.

   ○ C) A Roman gladius.   ○ D) A butter knife.

APPENDIX A: A GREEN GUIDE TO THE ZOMBIE APOCALYPSE

Going green seems to be one of the social rallying points of our society today, and so ~~to appease the environmentalist wackos~~ in order to be ~~politically correct~~ environmentally conscious, we the authors have compiled the following information to demonstrate how the rise of the zombies, while being a profoundly inconvenient truth, is in fact, a good thing for our mother Earth (Hack – cough).

TOP TEN REASONS WHY ZOMBIES ARE GOOD FOR THE ENVIRONMENT:

10) Zombies attack only humans leaving nature alone.

9) All zombies will eventually decompose, returning their organic matter to the soil.

8) Zombies do not breathe, belch, or fart, and so produce almost no harmful greenhouse gases.

7) Zombies will become carrion, providing enough of a ready food source that the California condor, and many other endangered scavenger species, will have an opportunity to make a complete comeback.

6) Zombies don't build single family housing, produce 2.5 children, have multiple pets, or drive SUVs by themselves in the carpool lane, giving them a minimal carbon footprint.

5) Zombies do not breed, resulting in zero population growth.

4) Zombies use no evil fossil fuels. In fact, with proper planning, they're likely to be the chief source of supply in a million years or so.

3) The technological engine of modern society will be effectively turned off, ending the human industrial threat to the Earth.

2) Nature will reclaim the now uninhabited spaces, ending urban sprawl.

1) As a direct result of the rise of the zombies, some 99% of the evil Earth destroying humans will have been eliminated.

APPENDIX B: GLOSSARY OF COMMON TERMS

Catastrophic crosshair moment: Any one single moment of stupidity that directly and inalterably leads to a person's demise.

Crosshair candidates: Anyone who, through action or attitude, proves that they are more likely to be a liability rather than an asset to the group. Someone for whom ending their life now may be the most merciful course of action.

Crosshairs: Slang expression, used often in exasperation, in reference to someone's act or statement of stupidity.

Crosshairs moment: An individual act of thoughtlessness, clumsiness, or misperception. What might in other circles be called a "blonde" or a "senior" moment.

Re-dead: The state wherein a zombie is rendered no longer un-live. *Re-deadly:* Anything that creates the potential to render a zombie re-dead. *Re-deadlier:* Anything having a greater potential to render a zombie re-dead. *Re-deadliest:* Even more re-deadly than re-deadlier.

Re-death: The moment that a zombie becomes re-dead and its state of existence thereafter.

Re-demise: See re-death.

Re-kill: Any action taken in order to render a zombie re-dead.

Shovel: An extraordinary useful survival implement, perhaps the single most useful survival tool a person can carry.

Two-hundred-forty-grain aspirin: A bullet to the head.

Un-life: The time period a zombie spends un-live.

Un-live: The state of zombification, wherein the victim is biologically dead yet still animated by the ZTA.

Un-living: All actions undertaken by a zombie in the process of their un-life.

Zom: A zombie, slang usage, (see zombie).

Zombie: The body of a dead person given the semblance of life.

Zombie apocalypse: The end of civilization as we know it, brought about by any zombie transforming agent (ZTA).

Zombie chow: Any individual, unfortunate, or crosshair candidate enough to be eaten by a zombie.

Zombie Transforming Agent (ZTA): Whatever catalyzing agent is responsible for the zombification of human beings.

Zombification: The act of, or process of transformation into a zombie.

Zombified: Having been transformed into a Zombie.

Zombism: The state or condition of being a zombie.

Zombology: The study of zombies.

Zomnabulate: To walk or perform any action while being a zombie. *Zomnabulated:* Having moved while being a zombie (e.g., The decaying corpse zomnambulated across the lawn.). *-lating,* (e.g., The zomnabulating heap stumbled off the edge of the cliff.). *-lates,* (e.g.The mindless horde zomnabulates with the appearance of unity.). *-lar,* (e.g. The shuffling, half asleep high school student was zomnambular in appearance.). *-lation,* (e.g. The research team created a video catalogue of the characteristics of zomnabulation.).

APPENDIX C: THE ZOMBIE APOCALYPSE SHOVEL BLADE COOKBOOK

We hold it to be an obvious fact that your shovel is about the most versatile tool you can have in your apocalypse survival gear. To prove this point, we have postulated the concept of using your shovel as a cooking implement. While we hope it is not often necessary to use it in this manner, to demonstrate its versatility in this regard, we have tested a number of recipes on our own shovel blades and now offer them to you.

In the spirit of creativity, we encourage you to experiment on your own, to develop shovel blade cuisine. We maintain that anything can be cooked on a shovel blade with a little thought and the application of some ingenuity.

Note: You do not need to wait for the apocalypse to put this valuable application to good use; it is a particularly useful camping methodology. With a standard mess kit, a roll of aluminum foil, your knife, a spatula, and a full sized shovel blade, you can prepare any number of tasty meals, without having to tote around pots and pans.

CHOOSING AND PREPARING YOUR SHOVEL

This might not be obvious, but you can't just grab any old shovel and start cooking on it. A little preparation is in order. First, a good cooking shovel is a full sized, ten-inch steel bladed shovel with a fully molded blade. Avoid riveted or screwed on blades or any blade coated with anything like zinc or chrome. Once you have selected your steel shovel, you will need to clean it and temper it. Manufacturers usually spray shovels with a rust-preventing lacquer before shipping so this will have to be completely removed. If it is not a new shovel, any rust spots should be cleaned away with sandpaper or steel wool, and if the owner was conscientious enough to rub down the blade with oil after each use to prevent rust, this will have to be removed as well.

Clean the blade thoroughly with dish detergent and hot water, using sandpaper or steel wool to remove any manufacturers' coatings. Once

the blade is cleaned and dried, rub it down with a common vegetable oil. This will prevent rust, as well as any petroleum-based product and will not be a problem for cooking later. Yes, it is true that a vegetable oil may go rancid in time, but any self-respecting apocalyptic shovel owner will certainly use their shovel far too often for this ever to be a problem.

To temper your shovel build a nice hot fire and hold the blade in the flames until the tip begins to glow. Be careful not to burn the handle. Once the blade is clearly hot throughout, thrust it in to a bucket of cool water. Now it is ready to cook on.

ALL-IN-ONE METHOD
For those of you who feel the above is a bit too much work, here is another method. Select a new shovel, remove the handle from the blade, build a fire, and throw the blade on the coals, allow the blade to heat to glowing from tip to handle shaft, then carefully pull it from the fire and plunge it into cool water. This will remove any coating completely. Reattach the handle or use without.

TECHNIQUES
Shovel blade cooking requires the development of a few techniques. Holding the blade level is one of the most important skills to acquire. When planning to cook on your shovel, it can be helpful to set aside three stones to set into the coals as a three-point shovel rest. For maximum heat, fill the space between the rocks with glowing embers. Spread the embers lower for better heat control. It is also a good thing to use a stick to hold the shovel handle in a resting position so that your shovel blade does not tip while you are cooking. The shovel blade cooking surface is very much like a wok, with a hot spot in the lowest area and graduated heat up the curved sides. At times, you will have to hold the blade turned slightly to one side or the other to create the largest cooking area for items like grilled sandwiches. With a little practice, you will develop your technique.

There are many sorts of shovels, with blades that may, in fact be arguably better for a task such as cooking. A broad, flat bladed coal shovel might be an excellent surface for making things like pancakes,

the flat blade being much more like a griddle surface. But, the idea here is survival, and the clearest shovel choice for survival is by far the standard spade shaped shovel, the ten-inch blade being the authors' undisputed favorite in the widest variety of survival applications. Therefore, this is the shovel of choice and the shovel considered in the preparation of the following recipes. Once you become one with your shovel, as any self-respecting survivor should, you will find there is Zen to shovel blade cooking. As a reader of this book, we guarantee you will survive the zombie apocalypse, and we wish you many happy and healthful meals, cooked on an open fire, in good company, on the well-tempered blade of your faithful shovel.

STAPLES

Whenever you are leaving your stronghold for a foraging mission and may need to stay overnight in an unknown place with unknown resources, it is advisable to prepare a cooking box for each vehicle. A large plastic storage tub works well for this purpose and has the advantage of a tight-sealing lid to keep out insects and vermin. For the same reason, all items contained in your travel larder should be kept in self-sealing containers. Here is a list of basic staples you should consider including:

- All-purpose flour
- Corn meal
- White sugar
- Brown sugar
- Honey
- Maple syrup
- Yellow and brown mustard
- Catsup
- Butter and or margarine
- Baking powder
- Baking soda
- Whole rolled oats
- Sesame or peanut oil
- Extra virgin olive oil
- Powdered milk

- Vanilla extract
- Ground cinnamon
- Ground ginger
- Ground nutmeg
- Garlic powder
- Chili powder
- Dried chilies
- Salt (preferably sea salt)
- Black pepper
- Ground oregano

- Canned soups
- Lemon juice
- Malt vinegar
- Tabasco/hot sauce of your choice

• Peanut butter (creamy or chunky, or both, your choice)
• Jelly or preserves, as available (grape jelly and strawberry preserves are both recommended.)
• Vegetable shortening

*Onions
*Potatoes
*Carrots
*Celery

*eggs

*Fresh vegetables, fruit, and eggs will be available only if you make the effort to provide them. Root/tuber vegetables are easy to grow and are hearty. They can be grown indoors in planter boxes, and most grow quite quickly. If you want eggs on a regular basis, you will have to plan to have chickens. This is not difficult, but like so much else, requires some planning on your part.

A Note About Eggs: If you do not pre-plan, or otherwise do not want to deal with chickens, you can substitute reconstituted powdered eggs in most of the recipes. They are generally fine in things like breads, crusts, and flapjacks, but they just aren't the same, and of course can't be used where a recipe calls for an egg with a yolk. However, if that's all you've got, enough other flavors can make them okay in a scramble.

It is important that you consider foraging trip meals ahead of time and pack in your larder what you anticipate you will need for your specific meals. However, it is recommended that you keep your staples in good order in case opportunity provides something unexpected. If you are inventive and not squeamish, road kill can make wonderful protein provisions and will allow you to create delightful meals on the fly. The best pheasant in orange glaze we ever tasted came right off the grill... the grill of our truck that is.

Most of the listed items will be readily available for the taking on supermarket shelves, or on the very shelves of your stronghold should

you choose the warehouse club store as has been suggested. Other items will require a bit more of you, but we assure you it is all well worth the effort.

So, now that you've gotten through the verbiage how about we get right to the shovel blade meals? Try them for yourself; we think you'll like them.

BREAKFAST:

BASIC EGGS –

Eggs are very easy to cook, and in fact are very easy to overcook. Too much heat for too long is the most common problem. Here is a simple process for crosshair candidate proof, shovel blade fried eggs.

Warm up your blade and add a heaping tablespoon of fat of your choice. Many people prefer to use the dripping from freshly cooked bacon, but any of your oils or butter will do. Heat until the oil is hot enough to sizzle a test drop of water. Break in two or three eggs. Remove the shovel from the fire as soon as the whites show their first indication of cooking at the edges. Baste the eggs with the hot fat for three or four minutes until each yolk films over. Serve with salt, pepper, and hot sauce if available, a nice side of bacon and a slice or two of toast are perfect accompaniments.

If you prefer your eggs scrambled, here is a simple trick that may make all the difference. The addition of milk to eggs for scrambling can have a tendency to toughen scrambled eggs. Instead, add a tablespoon of cold water for each egg. Mix the eggs and water with salt and pepper to taste. Then heat a little fat on your shovel blade (not hot enough to smoke just warm enough to sizzle water). Tip in the eggs; stir the eggs continuously until you begin to see some hardening then remove the blade from the heat and continue to stir until the eggs are cooked through. As they will continue to cook even once served, plate them while they are still creamy and soft.

BACON –
Too ardent heat is the enemy of wonderful bacon. Cooking more slowly over a milder heat will always yield better results. Start with your shovel blade cold. Lay your bacon strips out along the length of the blade. This is a good application for your three-point blade rest. Fry the bacon slowly over a few embers set between the stones. Turn the slices occasionally and pour off excess fat if you like them crisp. As with the eggs, it is better to serve bacon before it is cooked just as you like it, as it will continue to cook on the plate.

Note: If you like cooking with bacon fat then tip the fat into a handy can where it can be kept for future use.

OMELETS & SCRAMBLES –
Nothing is easier than turning a few fresh eggs into a delicious omelet or scramble. There are lots of inventive names for regional egg dishes based on themed available ingredients, so add what you have on hand and call it what you want.

Ingredients
- 2 eggs, or the equivalent reconstituted powdered eggs
- ¼ cup diced vegetables (usually of two types)
- ¼ cup diced mushrooms, or diced tomato if available
- ⅓ cup shredded cheese
- salt & pepper to taste
- Dab of margarine or butter

Directions
1. Place a dab of butter or margarine on your warm shovel blade. (If it smokes, it is too hot).
2. Beat your eggs with a little bit of cold water (1 tablespoon per fresh egg) and tip into shovel blade.
3. For a scramble, add all additional ingredients immediately and stir until eggs are creamy and well mixed. Serve when eggs look slightly underdone.

4. For an omelet, let eggs cook until the mass shows solid against the blade, but still uncooked on the top. Turn the mass of eggs and immediately add diced vegetables and cheese on top. Once eggs are firm fold over by half and serve.

Authors' personal favorite: Diced onions, green/red peppers, mushrooms, cheddar cheese, and ham.

FLAPJACKS –
Almost everybody's favorite!

Ingredients
- 1 cup all-purpose flour
- 1 teaspoon double action baking powder
- 1 teaspoon salt
- 3 tablespoons margarine or butter, softened
- 1 whole, fresh or dried egg
- ½ cup reconstituted dry milk

Directions
1. Add all your dry ingredients together in your mess bowl, cut in softened margarine or butter and add egg (fresh is better, reconstituted will do). Add milk slowly, stirring until batter is wet enough to pour easily. Add more or less milk to desired consistency. Thinner batter will give you thinner, but tenderer flapjacks.
2. Heat your shovel blade to medium, and then wipe it sparingly with bacon rind or a bit of butter. Do not let the metal reach smoking temperatures. Hold the blade at the angle to give you the flattest surface. Pour batter to make largest possible ovals on flat of blade. Turn each hot cake only once, when it begins showing tiny bubbles. The second side will take only about half as long to cook. Alternate sides of blade while cooking additional flapjacks.
3. Serve immediately with maple syrup or other favored toppings.

SPAM HASH –

Ingredients
- ¼-½ can Spam (diced)
- 1 medium onion
- 1 large potato
- 3 tablespoons margarine or butter, softened
- Dash salt
- Dash pepper
- Dash garlic powder (optional)

Directions
1. Add margarine or butter to warm shovel blade and let melt. Dice fresh onion and add to butter, allowing onions to cook to a nice wilt.
2. Peel and slice potatoes into quarter dices and add to cooking onions. Salt and pepper to taste. Cover with foil and allow to cook over gentle heat until potatoes are softened through.
3. Dice the amount of Spam desired and add to shovel blade. Add garlic at this time if desired. Stir gently allowing to cook until Spam pieces are caramelized along the edges.
4. Serve on your mess plate, or eat directly from the shovel blade.

ONE-EYED EGYPTIAN SANDWICH (EGG IN A HOLE OR EGG IN A NEST) –

Ingredients
- 1 slice bread
- 1 large egg (fresh, not powdered)
- 2-3 tablespoons margarine or butter, softened
- Dash salt
- Dash pepper

Directions
1. Make a hole in the center of your slice of bread. This can be done by simply pinching and tearing from the center until you achieve a hole slightly larger around than a typical egg yoke. Or, if you happen to have a shot glass, this makes a beautiful round hole by pressing its

open top to the center of the bread. Once you have made your hole, generously butter one side of the bread and place it butter down onto your pre-heated shovel blade.

2. Quickly butter the remaining side of the bread while it cooks on your blade. Once the down side shows evidence of light browning, flip over the bread.
3. Crack a fresh egg into the hole and allow it to spread slightly beneath the bread. Once the egg begins to show solid, flip it and bread as one and allow to cook on the opposite side. Add salt and pepper to taste.
4. Serve on your mess plate or eat directly from the shovel blade.

An option is to add a slice of cheese just before serving, this is called a *"one eyed Egyptian with a patch."*

LUNCH:

BASIC GRILLED CHEESE & OTHER GRILLED SANDWICHES –

Ingredients
- 2 slices bread (any available)
- Spreadable butter or margarine
- Sliced cheese (cheddar or American work best, but any sliced cheese will work)

Directions
1. Preheat shovel blade to medium heat. Generously butter one side of a slice of bread. Place bread butter-side-down onto one side of shovel blade and add one slice of cheese.
2. Butter a second slice of bread on one side and place butter-side-up on top of sandwich. Grill until lightly browned and flip onto opposite side of blade; continue grilling until cheese is melted.
3. Enjoy.

The real beauty of a basic grilled cheese is that it is the foundation for any number of tasty grilled sandwiches. Almost any sliced meat product goes wonderfully in a grilled sandwich. Change up the cheese and

experiment with sauces and extras, and a whole world opens up.

a. Chicken and bacon, grilled with a little Swiss or Provolone cheese, topped with some lettuce and tomato, and a bit of thousand island or ranch, yields a tasty club sandwich.

b. Pumpernickel rye, Corned beef, Swiss cheese, sauerkraut and thousand island creates a Ruben. Substitute chicken or turkey for the corned beef and you have a Rachel.

c. A little ham and Swiss cheese are a classic.

Experiment and you could become known as the shovel blade sandwich king. And, you can always prepare condensed soup in your mess cup for a tasty accompaniment. Who doesn't love a grilled cheese with a cup of tomato soup? That's classic comfort food, and during the zombie apocalypse, take any comfort you can get.

DINNER:

STIR FRY –

Ok, so stir fry can be so many things! Like a scramble, you can stir fry with whatever you happen to have on hand. It can be as simple as matching a given sauce to a set of ingredients, or as complicated as preparing your favorite specific regional Chinese dish. The thing is, the shovel blade, of all cooking implements is most like a wok and so any sort of stir fry is a natural for shovel blade cooking. If you are a fan of stir fry in general then we suggest you add a number of Chinese sauces to your larder, and get yourself a stir fry cook book for ingredient specifics and dish names. For survival purposes, it is easy to whip up a tasty stir fry using whatever you have on hand. Include such exotic ingredients as small game (i.e., squirrel, rabbit, raccoon, pheasant, etc.) or native greens such as dandelion, mint, cattails, or grass shoots. If you can manage to cook up a pot of rice to go with it, you can usually satisfy most any hunger.

So, rather than give one, or two, or twelve specific stir fry recipes, instead we'll suggest some common ingredients that seem to always fit the bill and give you some tips for crosshair proof stir fry on a shovel blade.

Typical Ingredients:

- Bamboo shoots (should be available in cans)
- Bean sprouts
- Beans (usually of the larger types, from a can)
- Bell pepper, any colors
- Bok Choy
- Broccoli
- Cabbage, of all types
- Carrots
- Celery
- Egg plant
- Eggs
- Garlic
- Ginger
- Green onion
- Mushrooms, fresh or canned
- Nuts, (peanuts and cashews typically)
- Onions
- Peas, or baby pea pods
- Tofu
- Water chestnuts (should be available in cans)

Sauces

Chinese sauces can vary quite a bit in flavor, but can generally be divided in to three types: 1) Dark, 2) Light, and 3) Sweet.

1) Dark sauces are richer and deeper in flavor and can be used on any ingredients; they are especially good with deep flavored ingredients like beef and other red meats. Not recommended for fish dishes.
2) Light sauces are generally milder and allow for ingredients with delicate flavors to come through. Recommended for fish dishes and milder meats, such as shrimp and chicken.
3) Sweet sauces, including typical Sweet and Sour are generally reserved for chicken, pork, and shrimp.

Shovel Blade Stir Fry Cooking Tips

1. Make sure you have everything you need before you start cooking! Never try to prepare ingredients while stir frying.
2. Always cut all the vegetables so that they will cook easily and be easy to eat (bite sizes).
3. Pre-heat your shovel blade before adding oil. Add the oil slowly drizzling it on both sides and the bottom of the blade. (Up to 3 tablespoons depending on the dish: peanut, canola, or other vegetable oil.) The oil heats faster this way.
4. Season the oil by cooking a few pieces of garlic or ginger. (Just watch your heat so that you don't burn it.)
5. Pre-cook your meat ingredient, and remove while cooking vegetables. Add it back in at the last so that it warms but does not over cook; doing this will help preserve individual flavors.
6. Add vegetables according to density. Heavier vegetables, such as broccoli, carrots, and eggplant require more cooking time. Add leafy vegetables last.
7. Wash and thoroughly drain vegetables ahead of time.
8. To add sauce, create a "well" by pushing vegetables and/or meat, up the sides of the shovel blade. Add the sauce in the middle and stir to thicken (cornstarch can be added as a thickener) before combining with the other ingredients.
9. Serve the stir-fried dish immediately.

Once you get the hang of it and a practical knowledge of sauces and ingredients, you will find that shovel blade stir fry is some of the easiest and indeed tastiest shovel blade cooking to be had. We suggest you apply your own creativity and give it a try. Who knows, send your favorite recipes to the authors and you might end up in the *"Shovel Blade Gourmet."*

HEARTY CHICKEN FRIED RICE –

Ingredients
- 1 egg
- 1 tablespoon water
- 1 tablespoon butter
- 1 tablespoon vegetable oil
- ½ large onion, chopped
- 1 cup cooked white rice, cold
- 1 tablespoon soy sauce
- ½ teaspoon ground black pepper
- ¾ cup cooked, chopped chicken meat

Directions
1. In your mess cup, beat egg with water. Melt butter in the base of the shovel blade. Add egg and let cook to solid. Remove from blade and cut into shreds.
2. Heat oil in base of shovel blade; add onion and sauté until soft. Then add rice, soy sauce, pepper, and chicken. Stir fry together for about five minutes, and then add in egg. Serve hot or eat directly from shovel blade.

STEAK & BURGERS –

Not to intentionally offend all you vegetarian-types out there, but what could possibly be better than sliced or ground cow combined with fire. We'll be the first to admit that a shovel blade might not be the preferred way to cook a steak or a burger. If you can come up with any sort of grill surface, use it, but shovel blade beef is every bit as good as a skillet fried steak or burger, any day.

The authors are not big proponents of adding anything to ground beef to make burgers, just add a little salt and pepper, form into patties, and cook on the blade about six minutes per side (depending on thickness). Serve with whatever burger fixings you happen to have.

For a good steak, grilled or blade fried, tenderize the beef if needed with a few good whacks from the back of your shovel blade. Be sure to let the steaks rest and come to room temperature before cooking (especially if the meat has been frozen).

Pre-heat your shovel blade, brush down the steaks with butter and add a little salt, pepper, and garlic powder. Cook about five or six minutes per side and flip only once, don't worry a steak with a lot of poking or prodding, just let it cook. A bit of browning on the outside with a rich pink center would be the authors' preference for doneness, but you cook it the way you like.

If you are fortunate enough to have steaks, bake a few potatoes as well. Just clean them, wrap them in foil (a couple thicknesses), and push them into the base of the fire embers, where there is heat, but no longer a lot of glow. These should be cooked in about forty minutes so set them up well before you cook your steaks. Sour cream may be hard to come by, but a little butter, goes a long way.

FISH –

If, by chance you have the time and opportunity to catch some fresh fish while out and about, they may easily be prepared on a shovel blade. There is nothing quite like a freshly caught fish cooked up flakey and tender.

To prepare your catch, gut and scale soon after landing. Trim fins but unless you object, leave on the head and tail, which contain the sweetest meats. For larger catches, fillet, or steak as appropriate. Keep your fish dry, cool, and well ventilated until it is time to prepare for cooking.

You do not want to dry out fish while you cook it, or turn it rubbery. Once the fish is easily flaked, it is done. Cooking at a medium heat, and only until the flesh is no longer translucent will keep the fish tender and moist. To bring out its delicate flavor, lightly salt the prepared fish inside and out, about an hour before cooking.

Cook directly on blade coated with a small amount of olive oil. Serve topped with a bit of fresh butter.

If you prefer a bit of coating roll your fish in flour, fine crumbs, or cornmeal and add a bit more oil to your blade. Brown the fish on both sides, remembering to remove it from the blade as soon as it is flaky throughout.

When serving add salt, pepper, lemon juice, or even malt vinegar to taste.

DESSERT:

APPLE DUMPLINGS –

Ingredients
- 1 lb. tart cooking apples
- ½ cup sugar
- Dash of ground ginger
- ½ cup water
- 1 tablespoon lemon juice
- ½ cup biscuit mix
- Splash of milk
- 1 tablespoon sugar mixed with ½ teaspoon cinnamon

Directions
1. Wash, pare, core, and thinly slice the apples. Place apples on shovel blade.
2. Add sugar, ginger, water, and lemon juice and stir well to combine.
3. In your mess kit cup, stir together the biscuit mix and milk just until mix is moistened.
4. Heat apple mixture to boiling.
5. Drop dumpling mixture in three portions over apples. Simmer, uncovered, for ten minutes.
6. Sprinkle with cinnamon and sugar. Cover with aluminum foil and simmer until apples are tender and dumplings are cooked through, about ten minutes longer.

This recipe works well with various fruits, try it with peaches, pears, plums, even mixed berries, alter sugar and ginger as needed to taste for a flavorful dessert every time.

SHOVEL BLADE BROWNIES –

Ingredients
- ⅝ cup sugar
- 1 large egg
- ½ cup all-purpose flour (spooned and leveled)
- 2 tablespoons powdered milk (heaping)
- 1 ounce cocoa powder
- Dash of salt
- 2 tablespoons (¼ stick) unsalted butter
- Dash of vegetable oil
- 4 ounces chopped dark chocolate, or chocolate chips

Directions
1. In your mess bowl, whisk together sugar and eggs.
2. In another bowl, whisk together flour, cocoa, and salt.
3. On shovel blade, bring butter and reconstituted milk to a simmer. Add chocolate, stirring constantly, until chocolate has melted, about one minute. Remove from heat, and let cool five minutes.
4. Add chocolate mixture to sugar mixture, whisking until blended (reserve shovel blade).
5. Fold in flour mixture. Pour batter into shovel blade.
6. Cover with foil and bake until a toothpick inserted in center comes out clean, about forty minutes. Serve from blade, warm or at room temperature.

Helpful Hint: Raid your larder for brownie mix-ins: pecans, walnuts, and chocolate chips are terrific.

CHOCOLATE CHIP COOKIES –

Ingredients
- 2 ¼ cups all-purpose flour
- 1 teaspoon baking soda
- 1 teaspoon salt
- 1 cup (2 sticks) butter, softened
- ¾ cup granulated sugar
- ¾ cup packed brown sugar
- 1 teaspoon vanilla extract
- 2 large eggs
- 2 cups chocolate chips (12 ounce package)
- 1 cup chopped nuts (optional)

Directions
1. Combine flour, baking soda, and salt in your mess bowl.
2. Beat butter, granulated sugar, brown sugar, and vanilla extract in second bowl until creamy.
3. Add eggs, one at a time, beating well after each addition.
4. Gradually beat in flour mixture.
5. Stir in chocolate chips and nuts.
6. Drop by rounded tablespoon onto ungreased shovel blade, usually two at a time.
7. Cover blade with foil and let stand over mild heat for nine to eleven minutes or until golden brown.
8. Remove blade from heat and allow to cool a couple of minutes.
9. Remove cookies to a wire rack to cool completely. (Oh who are we kidding, you haven't got a wire rack, and we know they are best still warm, so just eat them!)

Helpful hint: If you know you want to make cookies during a foraging trip, it is just plain easier to prepare the cookie dough ahead of time. Simply make the dough as you desire, shape into a log, and seal tightly in plastic wrap. That way, when it is time for dessert, you can simply take a piece from the dough log for the cookies and keep the rest safely in your larder. Kept tightly wrapped and out of the sun, the dough will be fine for several days even if it isn't always cool.

SHOVEL BLADE BAKING

Baking on a shovel blade is not the easiest prospect in the world, but with a little patience and practice, you will be surprised and pleased with your results. The key to shovel blade baking is controlling the heat so that things don't burn and they cook fairly evenly. Using your three-point stand (remember the rocks?) position hot embers around the stand but not close beneath the blade, and you will get better results. There is always the continuous movement method of heat control, which can yield nice results, but it's labor intensive and sometimes tiring. This is only recommended when everyone is cooking for themselves.

For even better baking results, get a piece of heavy wire mesh from a hardware store and cut it to fit across your shovel blade. Bend the edges carefully to grip the blade snugly and you have a nice baking rack. Use foil to create a dome over whatever you want to bake and set your blade down directly onto the embers, building the hottest embers around the sides. Using this method will give you wonderful baking results… but practice a bit first so you get the feel for heat control and baking times.

The recipes that follow are basic "pan" style, intended for direct on the blade cooking.

CORN BREAD –

Ingredients:
- 1 ¾ cups stone ground cornmeal
- ¾ cup all-purpose flour
- 1 teaspoon salt
- 2 teaspoons baking powder
- 1 ½ cups reconstituted powdered milk
- 1 large egg
- 4 tablespoons melted butter
- 1 to 2 teaspoons vegetable oil for the shovel blade

Directions:

1. In your mess bowl, combine the cornmeal, flour, salt, and baking powder. Combine well with a fork.
2. In your mess cup, stir together the 1½ cups of milk with the egg and melted butter. Add to dry mixture stirring with fork until blended.
3. Warm your shovel blade over flame or hot embers.
4. When batter is ready coat blade with vegetable oil swirling until blade is evenly and thoroughly coated. Spread the batter over the blade and cook manually over the coals until batter is firm and fairly even.
5. Using the basic shovel blade baking techniques, bake for ten to fifteen minutes until bread is firm and resilient to the touch.
   Serve as a welcome accompaniment to almost any meal, with butter and honey.

SIMPLE BLADE BREAD –

Ingredients
- 1 cup all-purpose flour
- 2 tablespoons powdered milk
- 1 teaspoon double action baking powder
- 1 teaspoon salt
- 3 tablespoons margarine or butter, softened
- Water

Directions

1. Add all your dry ingredients together in your mess bowl, cut in softened margarine or butter with a fork until mixture resembles coarse meal.
2. Heat your shovel blade to medium, and then wipe it with butter. Do not let the metal reach smoking temperatures. Add about ¾ cup of cold water to mixture to make a firm dough shape rapidly into two narrow oval cakes about one inch thick and place one on each side of blade.
3. Cook until crust begins to form and loosen from blade so that loaf does not stick. Once loaf is solid enough to hold together, turn loaf

and continue cooking until bread is an appetizing brown on both sides. This will take fifteen minutes to half an hour depending on heat.

4. When knife blade removes cleanly from center of loaf, remove from heat and let cool for three to five minutes depending on air temperature, and serve while still warm.

BISCUITS –

Ingredients
- 1 cup all-purpose flour
- 1½ teaspoons baking powder
- ¼ teaspoon salt
- 3 tablespoons vegetable shortening
- ½ cup reconstituted milk
- 1 tablespoon orange-juice concentrate (optional)

Directions
1. Preheat shovel blade to just short of smoking. Prepare a piece of foil to cover, allow room for slight doming.

2. In your mess bowl, combine the flour, baking powder, and salt. Cut two tablespoons shortening into the flour mixture using a fork until the mixture resembles coarse meal.
3. Add milk and juice concentrate into the flour mixture. Stir until a loose dough forms. Do not over mix.
4. To cook biscuits, coat the shovel blade with the remaining shortening. Drop heaping tablespoons of dough onto the hot shovel blade. Cover with foil and let the biscuits cook for two minutes. Move the shovel to a cooler section of the fire and let cook, covered, for twenty minutes. Turn biscuits over and cook for ten more minutes. Serve immediately.

So, now it's your turn. Get out there, test our recipes, and create a few of your own. When you come up with some great ones, send them to us, and we'll try them out ourselves.

APPENDIX D: RECOMMENDED RESOURCES

What follows is a list of material, both printed and film, that we advise you to study in order to be truly prepared. Keep in mind that this list should not be considered comprehensive or exhaustive. The following resources are just a few examples of the types of things you need to study in order to survive in a post-apocalyptic, zombie-infested world. We strongly suggest that you consult your local library, and of course, the internet for texts on these topics. If you can find texts that you prefer to the ones we've listed, by all means avail yourself of them.

ANIMAL HUSBANDRY

This may seem like an odd topic to include on this list, but eventually, you're going to want to eat fresh food. And if you're a meat eater, that means livestock. If you're going to have animals, you'll need to know how to look after them.

Animal Husbandry by Laura Zigman (Paperback - Mar. 2001)

Animals Make Us Human: Creating the Best Life for Animals by Temple Grandin and Catherine Johnson (Paperback - Jan. 12, 2010)

Big Book: Animals at the Farm / Animales de la granja (English and Spanish Foundations Series) by Gladys Rosa-Mendoza and Jason Wolff (Paperback - Apr. 1, 2009) - Large Print

Barnyard in Your Backyard: A Beginner's Guide to Raising Chickens, Ducks, Geese, Rabbits, Goats, Sheep, and Cows by Gail Damerow (Paperback - July 1, 2002)

The Complete Book of Foaling: An Illustrated Guide for the Foaling Attendant (Howell reference books) by Karen E. N. Hayes (Hardcover - Feb. 15, 1993)

How to Build Animal Housing: 60 Plans for Coops, Hutches, Barns, Sheds, Pens, Nestboxes, Feeders, Stanchions, and Much More by Carol Ekarius (Paperback - May 1, 2004)

Buffalo Book: The Full Saga Of The American Animal by David Dary (Paperback - Dec. 1, 1989)

Scientific Farm Animal Production (9th Edition) by Robert E. Taylor and Thomas G. Field (Hardcover - Aug. 5, 2007)

Sheep Book: Handbook For The Modern Shepherd, Revised & Updated by Ronald B. Parker and Garrison Keillor (Paperback - Aug. 15, 2001)

ANATOMY

Doctors will be extremely rare in the zombie apocalypse, so you'll want to have at least some basic knowledge of medical procedures. In addition to the texts listed below, you should include medical and pharmacological dictionaries and surgical procedural texts in your library.

Anatomy and Physiology for Dummies by Donna Rae Siegfried (Paperback - May 1, 2002).

Human Anatomy and Physiology with Interactive Physiology® 10-System Suite (8th Edition) by Elaine N. Marieb and Katja Hoehn (Hardcover - Jan. 10, 2009)

Principles of Anatomy and Physiology (Tortora,Principles of Anatomy and Physiology) by Gerard J. Tortora and Bryan H. Derrickson (Hardcover – 2000)

Anatomy and Physiology (Cliffs Quick Review) by Phillip E. Pack (Paperback - June 15, 2001)

Fundamentals of Anatomy & Physiology (8th Edition) [this set also includes: Atlas of the Human Body; and Interactive Physiology, 10 minute Suite] by Frederic H. Martini and Judi L. Nath (Hardcover - Apr. 5, 2008)

Anatomy and Physiology the Easy Way (Barron's E-Z Series) by I. Edward Alcamo Ph.D. and Barbara Krumhardt (Paperback - Nov. 17, 2007)

<u>Anatomy and Physiology: The Unity of Form and Function</u> by Kenneth S. Saladin (Hardcover - Jan. 5, 2009)

<u>Anatomy & Physiology</u> by Kevin T. Patton PhD and Gary A. Thibodeau PhD (Hardcover - Feb. 12, 2009)

<u>Anatomy & Physiology Workbook For Dummies</u> by Janet Rae-Dupree and Pat DuPree (Paperback - Sept. 4, 2007)

<u>Human Anatomy & Physiology (7th Edition)</u> by Elaine N. Marieb and Katja Hoehn Hardcover - Jan. 14, 2006)

AUTO REPAIR

Even if you're fortunate enough to have an auto mechanic in your group, chances are that he'll be very busy keeping your major machinery operating. Your vehicles will be vital to your survival, so you'll want to make sure that you can keep yours running whether you have a mechanic or not.

<u>Auto Repair For Dummies</u> by Deanna Sclar (Paperback - Nov. 17, 2008)

<u>How to Repair Your Car (Motorbooks Workshop)</u> by Paul Brand (Paperback - Oct. 15, 2006)

<u>The Complete Idiot's Guide to Auto Repair</u> by Vyvyan Lynn and Tony Molla (Paperback - July 3, 2007)

<u>The Complete Guide to Auto Body Repair (Motorbooks Workshop)</u> by Dennis Parks (Paperback - Aug. 15, 2008)

<u>Automotive Engine Repair & Rebuilding (Today's Technician) (2 Volume Set)</u> by Elisabeth H. Dorries (Misc. Supplies - Dec. 27, 2005)

<u>Auto Fundamentals (Text)</u> by Martin T. Stockel and Chris Johanson (Hardcover - Jan. 2000)

<u>Chilton's Auto Repair Manual, 1998-2002 - Perennial Edition (Chilton's Reference Manuals)</u> by Chilton (Hardcover - May 5, 2003)

How Cars Work by Tom Newton (Paperback - Oct. 11, 1999)

Auto Upkeep: Basic Car Care, Maintenance, and Repair by Michael E. Gray and Linda E. Gray (Paperback - May 1, 2007)

How to Diagnose and Repair Automotive Electrical Systems (Motorbooks Workshop) by Tracy Martin (Paperback - Nov. 10, 2005)

Dare To Repair Your Car: A Do-It-Herself Guide to Maintenance, Safety, Minor Fix-Its, and Talking Shop by Julie Sussman and Stephanie Glakas-tenet (Paperback - Aug. 30, 2005)

Automotive Technology: A Systems Approach by Jack Erjavec (Hardcover - Jan. 13, 2009)

CARPENTRY

Knowledge of carpentry will come into play when you're zombie-proofing your home, and also when you're modifying your long-term base. There's a bit more to it than simply knowing which end of the hammer to use, so a little study would not be amiss.

Black & Decker Complete Guide to Carpentry for Homeowners: Basic Carpentry Skills & Everyday Home Repairs by Chris Marshall (Paperback - Dec. 15, 2007)

Carpentry & Building Construction, Student Text by Mark Feirer, Feirer John, Mark Feirer, and Feirer John (Hardcover - Jan. 3, 2003)

Carpentry 5th Edition by Leonard Koel (Hardcover - Aug. 1, 2008)

Carpentry (For Pros By Pros) by Fine Homebuilding (Paperback - Apr. 3, 2007)

Carpentry by Leonard Koel (Hardcover - Sept. 1, 2003)

Carpentry & Construction, Fifth Edition (Carpentry & Construction) by Mark Miller and Rex Miller (Paperback - Oct. 20, 2009)

Homebuilding Basics Carpentry by Larry Haun (Hardcover - Apr. 1, 1999)

Measuring, Marking, and Layout: A Builder's Guide by John Carroll (Paperback - Oct. 1, 1998)

Modern Carpentry: Essential Skills for the Building Trade, Workbook by Willis H. Wagner and Howard Bud Smith (Paperback - Jan. 1, 2007)

Step-by-Step Basic Carpentry ("Better Homes & Gardens": Step by Step) by Better Homes and Gardens Books and Ben Allen (Paperback - Aug. 15, 1997)

Trim Carpentry & Built-Ins (Taunton's Build Like a Pro) by Clayton DeKorne (Paperback - Oct. 1, 2002)

ELECTRICAL WIRING

This is another one of those topics that's obvious when you think about it. After all, it wouldn't do electrocute yourself when trying to connect your generator to the main junction box, would it?

Wiring Simplified: Based on the 2008 National Electrical Code by H. P. Richter, W. C. Schwan, and F. P. Hartwell (Paperback - June 1, 2008)

Complete Wiring (Stanley Complete) by Stanley (Paperback - Feb. 5, 2008)

Electrical Wiring Residential by Ray C. Mullin (Paperback - Dec. 14, 2007) by Herbert P. Richter and F. P. Hartwell (Paperback - May 1, 2008)

Complete Guide to Home Wiring by Andrew Karre (Hardcover - Mar. 2001)

Electrical Wiring Commercial by Ray C. Mullin and Robert L Smith (Paperback - Jan. 14, 2008)

Wiring a House 4th Edition: Completely Revised and Updated (For Pros By Pros) by Rex Cauldwell (Paperback - Jan. 12, 2010)

Black & Decker Advanced Home Wiring: Updated 2nd Edition, Run New Circuits, Install Outdoor Wiring by Editors of Creative Publishing (Paperback - Dec. 15, 2008)

Ultimate Guide to Wiring: Complete Projects for the Home by Editors of Creative Homeowner (Paperback - June 1, 2007)

Residential Wiring to the 2008 NEC (Residential Wiring to the NEC) by Jeff Markell (Paperback - July 2008)

Wiring: Complete Projects for the Home by Editors of Creative Homeowner Barre and Clarke (Paperback - Apr. 15, 2004)

FIRST-AID

Like with the anatomy texts, these books will be very important when treating non-ZTA related injuries and illnesses. If your only medical knowledge is the administering of two-hundred-forty grain aspirins, your group population is going to shrink very fast, indeed.

FIRST AID FOR THE NBDE PART 1 2/E (First Aid Series) (Pt. 1) by Derek Steinbacher and Steven Sierakowski (Paperback - Nov. 12, 2008)

Wilderness Medicine, Beyond First Aid, 5th Edition by William W. Forgey (Paperback - Sept. 1, 1999)

American Medical Association Handbook of First Aid and Emergency Care by American Medical Association (Paperback - May 5, 2009)

First Aid for the Basic Sciences, General Principles (First Aid Series) by Tao Le and Kendall Krause (Paperback - Dec. 4, 2008)

Mountaineering First Aid: A Guide to Accident Response and First Aid Care by Jan D. Carline, Martha J. Lentz, and Steven C. MacDonald (Paperback - July 13, 2004)

The American Red Cross First Aid and Safety Handbook by American Red Cross and Kathleen A. Handal (Paperback - May 27, 1992)

First Aid for Babies & Children Fast by DK Publishing (Paperback - Dec. 25, 2005)

First Aid for the® Wards: Fourth Edition (First Aid Series) by Tao Le, Vikas Bhushan, and Julia Skapik (Paperback - Oct. 2, 2008)

First Aid for the Match, Fifth Edition (First Aid Series) by Tao Le, Vikas Bhushan, and Christina Shenvi (Paperback - Aug. 6, 2010)

First Aid for the Family Medicine Boards (FIRST AID Specialty Boards) by Tao Le, Christine Dehlendorf, Michael Mendoza, and Cynthia Ohata (Paperback - Nov. 20, 2007)

First Aid for the Pediatric Boards, Second Edition (FIRST AID Specialty Boards) by Tao Le, Wilbur Lam, Shervin Rabizadeh, and Alan Schroeder (Paperback - Jan. 19, 2010)

GARDENING

Like with animal husbandry, this topic will be very important for providing food to your group. What's more, there are many medicinal herbs that can be grown in a garden, so knowing how to do it just makes sense.

Trowel and Error: Over 700 Tips, Remedies and Shortcuts for the Gardener by Sharon Lovejoy (Paperback - Jan. 15, 2002)

Burpee : The Complete Vegetable & Herb Gardener : A Guide to Growing Your Garden Organically by Karan Davis Cutler, Cavagnarok David, Barbara W. Ellis, and David Cavagnaro (Hardcover - Nov. 10, 1997)

Gardening All-in-One for Dummies by The National Gardening Association, Bob Beckstrom, Karan Davis Cutler, and Kathleen Fisher (Paperback - Feb. 28, 2003)

The New York Times 1000 Gardening Questions and Answers: Based on the New York Times Column "Garden Q & A." by Garden Editors of the New York Times, Leslie Land, Dora Galitzki, and Linda Yang (Paperback - Jan. 15, 2002)

Carrots Love Tomatoes: Secrets of Companion Planting for Successful Gardening by Louise Riotte (Paperback - Jan. 2, 1998)

Lasagna Gardening: A New Layering System for Bountiful Gardens: No Digging, No Tilling, No Weeding, No Kidding! by Patricia Lanza (Paperback - Nov. 15, 1998)

Home Vegetable Gardening: A Complete and Practical Guide to the Planting and Care of All Vegetables, Fruits and Berries Worth Growing for Home Use (Forgotten Books) by Frederick Frye Rockwell (Paperback - Oct. 15, 2008)

The Vegetable Gardener's Bible: Discover Ed's High-Yield W-O-R-D System for All North American Gardening Regions by Edward C. Smith (Hardcover - Feb. 15, 2000) -

You Grow Girl: The Groundbreaking Guide to Gardening by Gayla Trail (Paperback - Mar. 2, 2005)

Gardening When It Counts: Growing Food in Hard Times (Mother Earth News Wiser Living Series) by Steve Solomon (Paperback - Apr. 1, 2006)

GUNSMITHING

This topic should require no explanation. Your firearms are your main defense against not only the zoms, but any other threats you may encounter. Related to this, we recommend learning how to hand load your own ammunition. There will be plenty available, but it never hurts to have a plan "B".

Gunsmithing (The firearms classics library) by Roy F Dunlap (Hardcover - 1996)

Practical Gunsmithing by American Gunsmith (Paperback - Apr. 1996) Gunsmithing - Rifles by Patrick Sweeney (Paperback - Oct. 1, 1999)

Do-It-Yourself Gun Repair: Gunsmithing at Home (Outdoorsman's Edge) by Edward Matunas (Paperback - Aug. 1, 2004)

Gunsmithing: Pistols and Revolvers (Gunsmithing: Pistols & Revolvers) by Patrick Sweeney (Paperback - Dec. 3, 2009)

Gunsmithing Made Easy by Bryce M. Townsley (Hardcover - Jan. 2006)

Home Workshop Prototype Firearms: How To Design, Build, And Sell Your Own Small Arms (Home Workshop Guns for Defense & Resistance) by Bill Holmes (Paperback - Nov. 1994)

Do-It-Yourself Submachine Gun: It's Homemade, 9mm, Lightweight, Durable-And It'll Never Be On Any Import Ban Lists! by Gérard Métral (Paperback - Sept. 1985)

.50-Caliber Rifle Construction Manual: With Easy-to-Follow Full-Scale Drawings by Bill Holmes (Paperback - Sept. 2002)

Professional Gunsmithing: A Textbook On The Repair And Alteration Of Firearms by Walter J. Howe (Hardcover - June 13, 2008)

Master Gunmaker's Guide to Building Bolt-Action Rifles by Bill Holmes (Paperback - Sept. 2003)

Gunsmith Kinks (Complete in 4 Volumes) (Hardcover - 2004)

OUTDOOR SURVIVAL

When you realize that during the zombie apocalypse, that all of the conveniences that we take for granted won't be available, the need for wilderness survival skills becomes obvious. In fact, they're as vital to you as your shovel.

Primitive Skills and Crafts: An Outdoorsman's Guide to Shelters, Tools, Weapons, Tracking, Survival, and More by Richard Jamison and Linda Jamison (Paperback - Aug. 17, 2007)

Outdoor Survival Guide by Randy Gerke (Paperback - Oct. 2, 2009)

Camping & Wilderness Survival: The Ultimate Outdoors Book by Paul Tawrell (Paperback - Mar. 1, 2006)

Outdoor Survival Skills by Larry Dean Olsen and Robert Redford (Paperback - Nov. 1, 1997)

Wilderness Survival by Gregory J. Davenport (Paperback - Apr. 30, 2006)

SAS Survival Handbook: How to Survive in the Wild, in Any Climate, on Land or at Sea by John Wiseman (Paperback - Mar. 2, 2004)

Survival Wisdom & Know How: Everything You Need to Know to Thrive in the Wilderness by CC The Editors of Stackpole Books (Paperback - Oct. 1, 2007)

The Boy's Book of Outdoor Survival: 101 Courageous Skills for Exploring the Dangerous Wild by Chris McNab (Paperback - Nov. 1, 2008)

SAS Survival Handbook: The Ultimate Guide to Surviving Anywhere by John Wiseman (Paperback - Jan. 1, 2009)

Wilderness Survival: Living Off the Land with the Clothes on Your Back and the Knife on Your Belt by Mark Elbroch and Michael Pewtherer (Paperback - Apr. 13, 2006)

Willy Whitefeather's Outdoor Survival Handbook for Kids by Willy Whitefeather (Paperback - June 25, 1997)

SAS Survival Handbook, Revised Edition: For Any Climate, in Any Situation by John Wiseman (Paperback - Mar. 3, 2009)

PLUMBING

Like carpentry and wiring, Knowledge of plumbing is one of those skills that will be necessary if you want to live a moderately comfortable life while waiting for the zoms to finally re-die.

Black & Decker Complete Guide to Plumbing: Expanded 4th Edition - Modern Materials and Current Codes - All New Guide to Working with Gas Pipe by Editors of Creative Publishing (Paperback - July 1, 2008)

For Pros by Pros Remodel Plumb by Rex Cauldwell (Paperback - May 1, 2005)

Plumbing Do-It-Yourself For Dummies by Donald R. Prestly (Paperback - Nov. 28, 2007)

Complete Plumbing (Stanley Complete) by Stanley (Paperback - Feb. 5, 2008)

Ultimate Guide to Plumbing: Complete Projects for the Home by Merle Henkenius (Paperback - Aug. 10, 2006) - Bargain Price

Plumbing (For Pros By Pros) by Rex Cauldwell (Paperback - Jan. 9, 2007)

Plumbing: An Illustrated Guide to the Plumbing Codes (Code Check Plumbing: A Field Guide to the Plumbing Codes) by Michael Casey mon, Douglas Hansen, Redwood Kardon, and Paddy Morrissey (Spiral-bound - Dec. 26, 2006)

Plumbing a House (For Pros By Pros) by Peter A. Hemp (Paperback - Oct. 1, 1994)

Basic Plumbing With Illustrations by Howard C. Massey (Paperback - Sept. 1994)

Plumbing Complete: Expert Advice from Start to Finish (Taunton's Complete) by Rex Cauldwell (Paperback - Sept. 2, 2008)

DEWALT Plumbing Professional Reference (Dewalt Trade Reference Series) by Paul Rosenberg (Paperback - Nov. 1, 2005)

WELL DRILLING

This information goes hand-in-hand with your plumbing knowledge. If you want running water, you'll have to get it from somewhere, right?

Water Well Drilling Troubleshooting Guide by mark crush (Paperback - 2005)

Wells and Septic Systems by Max Alth, Charlotte Alth, and S. Duncan (Paperback - Nov. 1, 1991)

Practical Well Planning and Drilling Manual by Steve Devereux (Hardcover - June 1997)

Well...What's All That Drilling About? by Andrew Stone, Jessica Bryan, and Rachel Pender (Paperback - Oct. 18, 2007)

Portable Water Well Drilling Rig Plans Book by mark Crush (Paperback - 2005)

The Home Water Supply: How to Find, Filter, Store, and Conserve It by Stu Campbell (Paperback - Jan. 10, 1983)

Drilling Engineering by J.J. Azar and G. Robello Samuel (Hardcover - Mar. 19, 2006)

Tapping Into Water Low Tech Well Drilling Techniques and Tools by Paul Sawyers (Paperback - Feb. 23, 2010)

ZOMBIE FICTION CINEMA

It's very important that you keep in mind that the films listed below are works of fiction. Nevertheless, we recommend viewing them, because despite the inventive nature of these works, their creators did manage to get some of the facts right, particularly in the areas of zom behavior and re-killing methods. Therefore, these films are worth your time (besides, who doesn't like a good zombie story?). There are probably some of you who are wondering why we didn't include the "28 Days/ Weeks/Months Later" films, "I Am Legend", "The Last Man on Earth", or "The Omega Man" on this list. Well, strictly speaking none of these are zombie movies. However, they're probably worth taking a look at because they do contain some valuable tips (of what not to do, if nothing else). Just remember, don't just watch them for their entertainment value, study them as though your life depends on it...Because that just might be the case.

Title	*Director*	*Year*
Army of Darkness	Sam Raimi	1992
Dawn of the Dead	George Romero	1978
Dawn of the Dead	Zack Snyder	2004
Day of the Dead	George Romero	1985
Day of the Dead	Steve Miner	2008
Diary of the Dead	George Romero	2008
The Evil Dead	Sam Raimi	1981
The Evil Dead II	Sam Raimi	1987
Flight of the Living Dead: *Outbreak on a Plane*	Scott Thomas	2007
George A. Romero's: *Survival of the Dead*	George A. Romero	2010
Land of the Dead	George Romero	2005
Night of the Comet	Thom Eberhardt	1984
Night of the Living Dead	George Romero	1968
Night of the Living Dead	Tom Savini	1990
Re-Animator	Stuart Gordon	1985
Resident Evil	Paul W. S. Anderson	2002
Resident Evil: *Apocalypse*	Alexander Witt	2004
Resident Evil: *Extinction*	Russell Mulcahy	2007
Resident Evil: *Afterlife*	Paul W. S. Anderson	2010

The Return of the Living Dead	Dan O'Bannon	1985
Return of the Living Dead Part II	Ken Wiederhorn	1988
Return of the Living Dead 3	Brian Yuzna	1993
Return of the Living Dead: *Necropolis*	Ellory Elkayem	2005
Return of the Living Dead: *Rave to the Grave*	Ellory Elkayem	2005
Shaun of the Dead	Edgar Wright	2004
Zombieland	Ruben Fleischer	2009

As previously stated, the above listed areas of study will be vital to the success of your survival plan. If you think that all this reading and movie watching is too much trouble, we have only one thing to say…you guessed it, "Crosshairs". We can't overstress how important preparation is. Surely, your survival, and that of your chosen group is worth cracking a few books and booting up the DVD player.

Once your studies are completed, your plans made, and your supplies and vehicle prepared, with this manual and your shovel in hand, you'll be able to live your life confidently, knowing that when the zombie apocalypse hits, you are well and truly prepared.

APPENDIX E: THE COMPLETE IDIOT'S GUIDE TO THE ZOMBIE APOCALYPSE

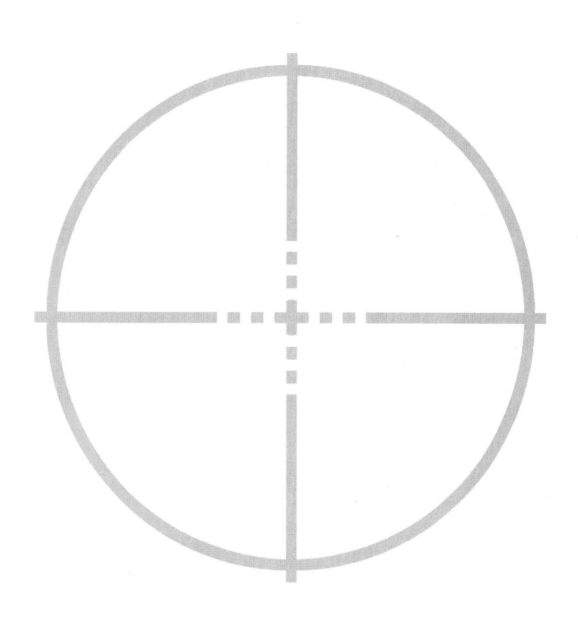

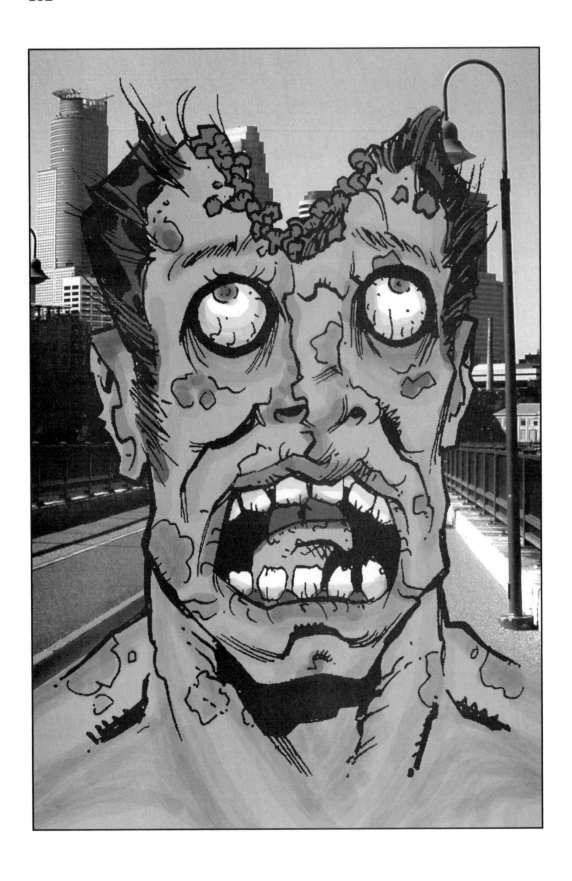

QUIZ ANSWERS

1) What is the best way to re-kill a zombie?

The correct answer is; C - shoot it in the head (3 pts). Decapitation will also work, if you don't mind getting that close (2 pts). Fire only works if you can trap the zom (1 pt). Poke it in the eye? Crosshairs (0 pts)!

2) What is your best zombie apocalypse vehicle?

The correct answer is; D - a 4WD SUV with a snowplow (3 pts). The tank might only work in the short-term (2 pts). A motorcycle only works as long as you can stay ahead of the zoms (1 pt). A boat is the crosshair choice (0 pts).

3) What term best describes a zombie?

The correct answer is; B - un-live (3 pts). The term undead refers to vampires and their ilk, which still retain a consciousness (2 pts). Re-dead only applies to re-killed zombies (1 pt). If you said mostly dead... crosshairs! Zombies are all the way dead (0 pts)!

4) What is your best long-range weapon?

The correct answer is; C - a rifle with a scope (3 pts). A handgun is effective, but the range isn't as great (2 pts). A bow's single shot capacity severely limits its effectiveness (1 pt). Only a crosshair candidate would pick a boomerang (0 pts).

5) What does ZTA mean?

The correct answer is; D - Zombie Transforming Agent (3 pts). If you picked any of the other options; crosshairs (0 pts)!

6) Which is your best improvised weapon?

The correct answer is; A - a sledge hammer (3 pts). A banjo has a tendency to break at inopportune moments (2 pts), and the golf club will bend after only a couple of hits (1 pt). As for the lawn mower... crosshairs (0 pts)!

7) Which is the best base camp?

The correct answer is; B - a warehouse club store (3 pts). A post office is only good for a night or two while travelling (2 pts). Your home is a short-term option at best (1 pt). Only squirrels and crosshair candidates live in trees (0 pts).

8) What is the best all-around tool to carry?

The correct answer is; C - a shovel-its possible uses are endless (3 pts). A crowbar is handy, but its usefulness is limited (2 pts). A pipe wrench would only help with crushing zom skulls (1 pt). A corkscrew?! C'mon, this is the zombie apocalypse not a wine and cheese party (0 pts)!

9) What is the best CD to use in a zombie lure?

The correct answer is; B - Michael Jackson's "Thriller" (3 pts). Led Zeppelin's "ZoSo" Has some good music, but not enough sustained back beat (2 pts). Yanni's "In celebration of life" has almost no beat at all (1 pt) and "Sounds of the rainforest" isn't even music! Crosshairs (0 pts)!

10) What is your best melee weapon?

The correct answer is; A - a katana (3 pts). It gives you the longest reach. The gladius requires much closer infighting (2 pts). Bowie knives are generally too short (1 pt). A butter knife is clearly ridiculous. Crosshairs (0 pts)!

The best possible score on this test is 30 points. If you scored 30 points, you are a true survivor. The zombie apocalypse will be a walk in the park for you. 20-29 points; you have a better than even chance of survival. Your outlook is good, but a bit more study and practice is in order. 10-19 points; you are one catastrophic crosshair moment from being zombie chow. If you're very lucky or have group members looking out for you, you might make it...but I wouldn't count on it. Less than 10 points; you are a complete crosshair candidate. Your chances of survival are so slim that when the zombies rise, you might as well just open the door and let them in.

MEET THE CREATORS

BUD HANZEL
Originally from Chicago, Bud has held a variety of jobs, including; security guard, home medical technician, retail store stock clerk, librarian and mail carrier. Unable to find success doing honest work, he decided to become a writer. He achieved some notoriety in the small-press comics field, writing for Now Comics, Big Bang Comics and Sundragon Comics. After having a dream about zombies overrunning the world, he knew that he had a duty to help humanity survive the zombie's attack. With this book, he hopes to accomplish exactly that. He lives in Minnesota with his cats, Nemo, Nala and Ashcan.

JOHN OLSON
Raised in the Minneapolis area, John has travelled extensively through Europe and Central America (the latter courtesy of the U.S. Air Force). After his stint in the Air Force, he enrolled in and later graduated from Iowa State University with a Masters of Fine Arts degree in graphic design. His checkered career includes; typesetter, production designer, frame store manager, editor-in-chief of a small press comic book company and college professor (some of his students even learned something). Sharing Bud's concern about impending zombie attack, he co-authored this book to help ensure humanity's continuation. He lives in Minnesota.

MARK STEGBAUER
Mark grew up on the West Coast, scribbling drawings on every piece of paper he could lay his hands on. He eventually became one of the comics industry's most accomplished and respected inkers. He has worked with just about every penciller in the field and has inked virtually every major character. His first foray into penciling and inking was on the critically acclaimed "Four Uncles of the Apocalypse". He has long known about the coming zombie apocalypse, and illustrated this book in an effort to get the word out to the masses. He lives in Eastern Wisconsin.